Yasmin Alibhai-Brown was b̶ Britain in 1972. She did her M̶ then taught for a number of years ̶ ̶ ̶ ̶ turning to journalism. She was the race editor for the *New Statesman and Society*, now works as a freelance journalist and has written for the *Guardian*, *Observer* and *Independent*. She also broadcasts on radio and television, mainly on race issues and co-authored, with Anne Montague, *The Colour of Love: Mixed Race Relationships*. She lives in London with her family.

NO PLACE LIKE HOME

Yasmin Alibhai-Brown

Published by VIRAGO PRESS Limited 1995
20 Vauxhall Bridge Road, London SW1V 2SA

Reprinted 1995

A CIP catalogue record for this book is available from the British Library

Typeset by Deltatype Limited, Ellesmere Port, Cheshire

Printed and bound in Great Britain by Cox & Wyman Ltd, Reading, Berkshire

For all those Ugandan Asians and Africans dispersed across the world.

For my son, Ari, and daughter Leila, so they can learn a little of who they are. For my husband Colin whose love and faith gave me yet another new beginning. For my father although it is too late, and most of all, my dearest mother whose life story will, I hope, be an inspiration.

Acknowledgements

I am indebted to so very many people. I owe my brother and his family and I know, alas, it is a debt I can never repay. My heartfelt thanks to Bhabhi, and the other Alibhais who gave me so much love for such a long time. I thank Sky for the life we had and for the son he gave me. Perhaps this will help him understand why there were so many tears. My thanks too to Zarina, Mick and Allegra for keeping our family connections going.

For the memories and support they gave me, I thank my childhood friends Lily Amarnani and Nazira Vayya; our neighbours Ma, the Patels and the Desais, and others too like Moss and Poss and Nurumasi. My many cousins, uncles and aunts whose lives were for so long tied in with ours, I thank them too. I recognise the excellent education imparted to me by my teachers at Kololo and later my tutors at Makerere. My thanks to all my Ugandan friends, especially Sophie Kafero and those who left as refugees and still keep in touch from wherever they are. Without these contacts, the past would, by now, have disappeared. I also know that the truly hard times would have been unbearable without my best friend Feriyal. And without the guidance of Bhikhu Parekh, I would have understood so much less than I do about the complexities of an uprooted life. My gratitude to Jafar Kareem, who when alive gave me so much strength.

I would like to acknowledge with love, the many white Britons who have helped to make me feel that I do belong: among these are those few who showed some faith in me at Linacre College, Oxford, and others like Kathy Gyngell, Brean and Ann Hammond, Jenny Swallow, Simon and Patty Brewster, Caroline and Jo Gipps, Yvonne Roberts, Len Brown, the Blaschkos, Jonathan and Elena Kingdon, my mother-in-law Vera Brown who has accepted me without reservations, and my dear chum, Anne Montague.

My thanks to Ruth Petrie who first asked me to write this book; to the Society of Authors for their support and to Melanie Silgardo, my editor, whose invaluable suggestions stopped this being an act of self-indulgence.

Finally I would like to state my eternal gratitude to Uganda, the country of my birth, to Britain where my two children were born and to the Indian subcontinent which somehow still manages to influence the way we live our lives.

Preface

No Place Like Home has been written with some trepidation. I have heard the objections and thought about the many reasons why a book like this should not be written. Don't disturb the memories of the dead or even the living, say my mother and my son. Let them be embalmed now in the good reputation that time brings to all but the most evil in the world. And anyway, the truth about families should remain within our own four walls. But the people who jostle for space in my head, both alive and from the other side, mean so much to me, I can't simply let their stories turn to dust.

There are the bigger ambitions too in the writing of this book. For the sake of our children, we need now to explore honestly our history and by telling it, give it substance. There are so many of us who feel we came from nowhere and are going God knows where, as bits of what we were fade away and what we have become seems hopelessly inauthentic. We need to describe how it all started over a hundred years ago when our forefathers arrived in Uganda from undivided India, and why we now find ourselves living in Britain, our sons and daughters only dimly aware of that place called Africa.

For the sake of those who are dying too. The elders in our community who carry the world they used to know with them when they go, some of them deeply hurt that so few were interested in their memories as they were reaching the end of their lives. Many are buried in this country where they still say we are aliens, and where even some of our graveyards get desecrated. Our graves in Uganda remain sacred and safe and yet when they threw us out of there there was dancing and singing in the streets.

Many people feel it is wrong to talk openly about how shamefully we often behaved as a community. It will give us a bad name. That would surely be treachery. But we must. How else do we earn the right to protect ourselves in this hard, unyielding place? Others are anxious not to offend the black leaders of Uganda and the British, who, after all, gave us a home. It is the unease of a dispossessed people who have never had a spot on earth to call unequivocally their own.

But this is also a celebration. Of my people who are survivors. Of Uganda, the people and the lovely country we were fortunate enough to know at least for a part of our lives and of those Britons who helped to ease the pain of exile, many of whom have been persuading me for years to write down the extraordinary journey which brought us all here.

Yasmin Alibhai-Brown
1995

PART I

1955–1961

We pretended to be real, to be learning, to be preparing ourselves for life, we mimic men of the New World, one unknown corner of it, with all its reminders of the corruption that came so quickly to the new.

V.S. Naipaul,
The Mimic Men

1

Japan flung himself on the red dry dust, wailing and raging against the malevolent aeroplane with such dazzling passion that he upstaged us all again.

His shrieks drew the attention of a policeman who loved watching planes through the wire fence at the small airport at Entebbe and who felt personally affronted by the curses that Japan was hurling at the roaring machine. He ran up to Japan waving his baton, threatening immediate arrest if the wailing didn't stop. Thwarted in a way I had never seen him before, Japan carried on sobbing quietly, head in his arms, dripping bloody tears as the red earth combined with the extraordinary stream of water pouring out of his huge brown eyes. Now, Japan was adept at the dramatic response. He could throw up a fit of pathos at any excuse, especially if my mother, whom he adored, reproved him for drinking, failing to arrive back from leave on time (ever) and squandering the meagre wages she was able to pay him to help her with the catering she was forced to do for weddings and religious feasts. But this was the real thing, arising from a deep font of despair. My brother, the love of his impoverished, circumscribed, life, was leaving for England.

Japan was our African servant, who was seriously underpaid, even by the appalling standards of the time. He made up for this by establishing for himself a unique position in our home and by selling his own distinct mango and lemon pickles to anyone

3

who came to visit. Tall and impressive, he had unusual chocolate brown skin, which he claimed, jokingly, must have come from having Asian blood. Nobody laughed at this. By the mid-fifties, such a thing had already become too horrible to contemplate, although in the thirties and forties it had been perfectly acceptable for early Asian pioneers and explorers to take up with black women.

He had been with us for years; cooking and cleaning for us, and protecting us from all that so easily threatened a peculiar and irregular family like ours. Inexplicably poor most of the time and even more inexplicably (relatively) rich for fleeting periods in between when my brilliant but impetuous father made something work for a while, we were well and truly the misfits in a community which painstakingly built a careful hierarchy based on accumulated wealth. We had no other history, having somehow landed in East Africa, an assortment from the subcontinent, carrying dreams, hopes and the heavy responsibility to make good whatever the cost. Caste and religious militancy had become lukewarm with the crossing of the seas and even during the barbarous killings of Partition, there was little lasting animosity between the different groups. At the beginning it was the indentured labourers who came, to build the railway and to escape the endless destitution which land reforms during the Raj had brought upon their lives. 'Slavery with pocket money' was how one of my more revolutionary Asian teachers described it. They came because famine and colonialism had dispossessed them of everything and they came because they were promised land which most were never to get. They were humble folk, poor and exploited like the Africans were. Many had been lured by wily agents who had offered the world in exchange for a thumbprint on papers which bound them for years and which most, being illiterate, couldn't understand. Need made them break the taboo of crossing the 'black water', the Kala Pani which they believed would eventually bring evil into their lives: a

4

superstition which in retrospect seems to make thoroughly good sense.

The country was slowly opened up as tracks began to connect villages and the road in from the Kenyan coast, where people arrived in their boats, began to be negotiated with a little safety. Wild animals were rife then and the preying, grasping strangers, white and brown, who assumed they had a right to establish themselves wherever they wished were not always greeted with smiling faces by the indigenous populations. But the interior was mysterious, enticing, full of possibilities, especially for the adventurous and ambitious. When they reached it they could not have been anything but wholly elated and intimidated.

Uganda, with its moist and raging green everywhere, prodigious, boisterous flowers, trees and grasses, and beautiful red earth. Utterly untamed. And the overpowering smells, especially from the waxy pink and white frangipani flowers, the white jasmine bushes, and in the evening the 'rat-ki-rani' – queen of the night – shrubs which breathed out a scent that filled the streets and your head. No wonder Uganda was only ever a protectorate, never comfortable enough to be a colony. Kenya was different. Away from the stark plains, you could see that it could be made to look more like the landscapes white Europeans had left behind. Ugandan foliage is altogether more rebellious, although the English administrators had some success in Entebbe, where they built their imposing state house and created a 'botanical garden' overlooking Lake Victoria. Here, flowers and trees had perfect neat circles of soil around them and even labels with interminable Latin names. They were taught their place.

The animals were less obliging. Once, as the Primus stoves were heating our picnic biriyani under one of these cultivated trees – something the keepers would not have approved of – a python who had just swallowed a goat started shuffling around one of the branches with irritation. Thirty of us, including my terribly overweight chacha Ramzan and chachi Remat had to

5

flee. They probably moved more and further on that day than ever before or since. Flab on the body was just one more symbol of gathering affluence and growing importance. Inches of floating ghee on food was another. From time to time, chacha and chachi were rich enough to have the lard removed from their vast stomachs. Chacha Ramzan described the operations in graphic detail after we had settled under another tree as he was loudly sucking the fat and gristle off a piece of mutton.

The children often shrieked with delight and terror when dipping in the lake water. Stepping on crocodiles and snakes, finding spouting hippos swimming by was commonplace. As were rabid dogs and evil-looking cats. We were taught to respect, but never, ever to trust any animal, tree or plant.

Imagine my shock when I saw, for the first time in England, not only human beings kissing dogs and cats, but gardens that were perfectly obedient and grass which was not furiously and radiantly green but gently so, so it was actually comforting to the eyes. I recently gave my English mother-in-law a jasmine plant from Marks and Spencer's. In a few days she had thrown it away because she could not bear, she said, the rotten, strong smell that permeated her bungalow in Shoreham-by-Sea. I understand exactly what she means. The quiet subtleties of English vegetation do not prepare you for the wildness of the tropics. I wonder if the early pioneers from this country actually loved Uganda for the way it shook up their senses. I wonder too how much I might have become part of this gentle beauty now and whether I might now find the country I was born in revolting and feral because of its undomesticated excesses.

But, whatever was frightening or even repulsive about it, the fascination with Uganda continued. After the first wave, the sharp, self-denying dukawallah started to appear, running his small dusty shop in the middle of a village, often alone, always sullen, suspicious and frightened, the only Asian for miles, selling oil, flour, matches and the much-coveted green Palmolive soap bar. These traders led simple lives, learned the local languages and had the trust of the Africans, who would often leave money in the safe keeping of the *wahindi* and get the kind of credit that so many of them living in abject poverty constantly needed. They had been forcibly moved into a commercialised world which they did not understand, so it was easy to exploit their bewilderment and confusion without even appearing to do so.

Behind the sparse accommodation, the dusty shop, the greasy shirt, the *wahindi* was building up his piles of money which bit by bit created greater and greater distance between him and the Africans around him. The inequality that had been symbolic and epitomised by skin colour now began to assume a reality. Was there ever real and equal respect even in those early days or was it merely commercial expediency, as it is today with the white businessmen of liberated South Africa? I don't know. They say there was. 'These black *shenzis* don't know how to make money, you know. It grows on trees here,' said my unbeloved chacha Ramzan when talking endlessly about how he was already in 1942 a millionaire, a mere ten years after he had arrived.

As time went by, a larger and slightly more self-indulgent community began to build up in the developing towns, now selling cars, radios, china, silks and brocades and jewellery – the bigger and more garish, the better. Asians bought these and stuffed them into cupboards. Hardly ever used, each new item gave them comfort that it had all been worth it. There were always more cupboards than chairs and tables in sitting rooms. Groaningly full, they had tiny glass windows which guests could peer through and see the piles growing and at least three padlocks to keep out the black hands of the servants, who were always presumed to have thieving dispositions even after they had devoted their lives to the family for decades. Japan knew he was treated differently. There was also nothing to steal in our house.

My mother always said she didn't want any of the things all those around her had. Gold and brocades, she said, what did they matter? But when her rings were stolen on one cold, frightening day in Shepherd's Bush, rings she had saved up to buy for thirty years, rings she was too old really to wear by then, how she sobbed, for days confessing how all her life she had wanted to be a cherished doll like her friends were. Meherunbai, standing tall, proudly dressed by her husband and put on display every Friday when the crowds gathered outside the mosque. Him fussing over her, straightening her hair, her imported pearls, as we all looked, breathless with admiration. Or Zora Masi whose arms you could hear long before she appeared with her massive clanging bangles.

Kampala, the main town, grew as more people from rural areas began to move in. Two parallel roads made up the commercial spine of the town. Here, bit by bit, Asians opened up their small shops. Interspersed with these dark, overstuffed, airless hovels (why bother with electricity and display, bloody waste of money) would be the elegant, spacious European shops with hardly a customer in sight. General Motors, Drapers, wonderfully forbidding dress shops which all went purple with patriotic pleasure during the coronation, when even the haughty white shopkeepers handed us sweets with little smiles. These moments of togetherness were contrived and rare. Apartheid, the discreet sort which did not need to proclaim itself with crass notices, was quietly established.

The Europeans lived up on the most beautiful surrounding hills. They had their own schools, clubs and menacing hedges and fences. Dogs too, who would bark if an unknown black or brown person wandered into the area.

Asians, who could afford it, then claimed the next-best bits, slightly lower down the hills of course, to establish their territories in the desirable suburbs. Their dogs would only bark at unknown blacks.

Blacks kept no dogs.

When the *wazungu* (whites) left, there was a scramble by rich Asians and powerful blacks to move up the hill. One Asian who had built at the highest point of the highest hill was the first to have his house confiscated when Asians were being targeted by Idi Amin.

Thrift, delayed gratification (maybe even delayed into the next world) ownership, endless hours in the shop, were the fundamental qualities which defined the Asian community. That and an immutable belief in their supremacy over the African and their subservience to the European except when it came to sexual morals, when there wasn't much to choose between the whites and blacks. The African, who worked in our homes and shops for fifteen hours a day for a pittance, according to our own convenient mythology was feckless, spendthrift and, most of all, unable to save. Papa was all of these things, which was very confusing. Africans were destined to be poor; 'It's in their nature, you know,' said chacha's son, my pompous cousin, Shamsu who had a body smell like rancid butter and who soaked his insides with neat whisky every night, went off to his black mistress and then regained sobriety and self-control by beating up his wife or his servant with a coat hanger. 'Bloody empty-headed, can't work, just want to drink their money, only understand the stick and the shoe. No culture, you know, not like us.' Papa thought Shamsu was a fool and a boor but he had money, so he got to sit in a special place in mosque reserved for the significant. Papa never went to mosque, having been excommunicated at the age of fifteen for objecting to special carpets being provided for 'these rich swines'. He could have got back on to the straw mats with an apology and a small offering, but he chose proudly to stay out and stand outside instead, a gesture that became meaningless as time went on because it was no longer even noticed by anyone.

We were a small, oddly elitist and esoteric Shia Muslim community which is led by the Aga Khan. At that time it was the grandfather of the present Aga Khan who was the spiritual leader. He had, in a short time, succeeded in modernising religious practice so that the mosque became a place for family rather than male worship. It had also started to become a place where you displayed your wealth through what you wore and how much you bragged outside the hallowed hall of worship. Women spent hours dressing up on a Friday, and those who could afford it chopped off their long hair and got themselves bouffants which hairdressers had to pump up with beer rinses and hairspray. The smell of stale beer, penetrating perfume and the dazzling array of saris gave the mosque a peculiarly decadent atmosphere, though it has to be said that the faith of the believers was beyond question. Pretending that we were going to pass out was one of the excuses we children used when we wanted to escape the serious business of praying and go and play hopscotch on the cool paving stones outside.

Papa would rant: 'Bloody idiots, what is this mosque of yours, a fashion club? Look at these ridiculous clothes. I tell you this is a joke. Have any of you read the Koran? Idiots, hypocrites . . .' At moments like this I would burn with shame and wish he would go, disappear like they said he always used to for years on end. I knew I would not miss him. I never have.

Poverty among Asians was an unspeakable disgrace (except for widows whom the rich baled out whenever they wanted to feel magnanimous or when old age necessitated an investment to gain a place in heaven). Sporadic poverty like ours, in a family led by a man who was clever, who read books and who had been in England for years, was no good to anyone, even during the terrifyingly bad times. Then my mother, covering her shame with conceit ('I would kill my children before begging for money from these people') would go behind some closed door and emerge with goods or a little money to see us through to the next time. After one of these expeditions she would cry as if she had been physically violated. But once the sorrow had lifted, she would choose to see it as a special privilege she had bestowed on the person who had helped to feed us for the next fortnight.

In his life Papa had unsuccessfully owned a bookshop, half a coffee shop, two restaurants, and the entire contents of Robert's of Bond Street's hat shop, which he had bought on impulse when ex-pats started receding back to the motherland, when the Mau Mau troubles in Kenya persuaded them that they were not, after all, invincible. The hats were stored in huge boxes in the back veranda of the small flat. When Papa got bored with the idea of making money on them – just who did he think was going to buy these hats? – the children in the neighbourhood started sneaking them out and wearing them, pretending to be English ladies. I was particularly fond of a purple velvet hat which had a long feather and a brooch with the silhouette of a fancy lady in a bustle. I also loved another brooch with a pearl border and a painted scene from a perfect English garden. I gave that to myself as a present from my father.

Papa had also been a car salesman, an insurance salesman and an importer/exporter. He had the brains to make it work, but no staying power and no real interest in the money he could make. He gave away things, never chased up those who owed him. Not because of kindness or generosity – that only happens when you value what you give away – but because he genuinely didn't value material things. His own needs were particular and not excessive; he left it to his wife to provide for herself and the children and him, and then devoted himself to grand illusions. It was hard not to despise him for the games he played and the pain he caused us all. But it was equally hard to despise him, because he was truly a dreamer. I only wish I had understood his dreams better.

The problem with Papa was that, unlike most other fathers in Uganda, he did not stick at any one job or business long enough to provide us with a secure base, and since he also never told us what was going on, good or bad, there was no way of preparing for the times when suddenly there was no money at all in the house, so my mother was always worried. The same sense of peril would be felt when there was an unexpectedly large amount of money around because this is when Papa lost all restraint and good sense.

Like the time Amir was sent off. Papa had made some huge commission from a transaction as a broker. He had been the intermediary in the sale of a hotel near the Rewenzori mountains. In 1994, a man from Uganda came looking for my mother to give her a few hundred pounds for shares my father had bought in this hotel all those years ago in her name. Her conviction that, in spite of everything, he did appreciate her, was confirmed by this invisible act of love so many years ago.

With money spilling out of his pockets, he came home to announce his decision. Amir, my brother, was going to England to find enlightenment, just as my father had done as a young man escaping the 'barbarity' of Pakistan. He hated his country because in his eyes it was not civilised and later because he felt it was smeared in the blood of those who had died during Partition. Oddly though, he had a sneaking regard for Mohammed Ali Jinnah whose cold, intellectual demeanour appealed to my father. He respected India more and he registered this fact by giving up Kutchi, his family language, and speaking in Gujarati. Most of his friends were Hindu too. His parents were to die without ever seeing their son again. He was oddly heartless without being unkind. 'Not a bad man, Kassam, you know my dear. Brainy too. But so irresponsible, a little mad you know, like all brainy people. Just doesn't care. Not a family man. Can't understand sending his son to UK. No food in the house sometimes. Poor wife. Simply can't understand the man,' chacha Abdul, another one of my father's rich and rotund cousins, pondered as he watched my father pacing alone, a tall lanky man with clothes flapping and always too short on the arms and legs and a cigarette in his mouth. This was not his scene. Fifty relatives and friends all carrying boxes of sweetmeats for the boy, consoling my mother as if at a bereavement. 'These people are stupid,' he grumbled. 'Uneducated, they know nothing. Do they think I want my son to write account books?'

Zarina (or Didi, as I called her), my sister, ten years older than me and a year younger than Amir, stood with him, intensely jealous that her brother was getting to go, but half glad that he was out of the way so she could have his bed in the sitting room finally. I adored my brother – adoration that was to cause me unspeakable pain in later years. He reciprocated, at least then. There was little in my arrival that threatened him. For my sister the birth of a sister was more ambiguous. On the one hand there was a live doll to dress, bathe and pinch. On the other hand, I think she feared that the unique place she occupied in my father's heart would have to be relinquished by the arrival of another daughter. She need not have worried. All the rooms in my father's heart were taken up or shut down by the time I was born.

'What will I do?' cried my mother pitifully. A complete contrast to my father, she was short, chubby and overwhelmingly warm. 'The boy has asthma. Never left me before, he's weak, he's a child. This madness your father has about that country, it will kill my Babu.' She was clearly not describing the Amir I knew, the dude who smoked heavily, smashed cars that he persuaded rich teenagers to steal from their parents and who could dance a mean dance when my father, who hated music, was out. Such is the love a mother can feel for an only son. Love with the power of blind faith behind it. I look at them now and I realise that my mother still doesn't know my brother (he is fifty-six) and cannot face the truth about him. Sometimes I wonder what caused my brother the greatest damage: the fact that my father never once clasped him to his heart or the blind infatuation that my mother has for him. An infatuation that Japan, who had no son of his own, shared.

Amir's departure scene at the airport was going on interminably with Japan now shouting out his fears in Swahili: 'Mama God has taken Amiroo. No good will come of it. You'll see now. It's very bad over there. Whites are evil over there. What shall we do, Mama?' Japan also believed, among other things, that whites captured blacks on Christmas Day and drank their blood, so he could not be entirely trusted on these matters.

Encouraged by Japan's deep anguish, my mother was building up to a fine climax. She was weeping copiously and beginning to wail while recounting the various frustrations of

13

her life, wondering how it was that she had managed to survive them and asking how she could possibly cope with this, the loss of her only son who had seemed altogether too pleased to get on that plane and get away from her to the place they all wanted to go to these days, London.

The money Papa made was spent not to move into a bigger flat or even catch up on the rent of the present one – which had one bedroom where we all slept except for Amir, who had made the tiny sitting room his own and where he slept when he bothered to come in late, to avoid the endless rows with Papa. Not even to buy a new mattress to replace the old one which smelt of many years of baby urine and much else besides and which my mother failed to freshen even with sprinklings of expensive Johnsons' Baby Powder, which we could ill afford. The smell still lingers in my nostrils. And the cold metal on my back as I slept between my parents until I was way past puberty. Two metal beds joined together with thin mattresses would part and I would sink in between, hating it and the snoring in my ears peppered with babble from my father whose brain never seemed to sit down and rest quietly a little. Domestic expenses were deemed by my father to be too petty for his attention or these occasional bouts of money. This responsibility he had magnanimously handed over to my mother. When he did earn money, therefore, my mother had no qualms about helping herself to whatever she could find in his pockets and wallets. He never knew how much he had and so did not pine over how much he had lost. She would hide the notes in the cups of her bra, and then when the perspiration on them had dried, store them in wrapped hankies in the folds of her saris. Afraid, always afraid that the next time he was broke, Papa would come looking and begging for some cash. It all balanced out and my parents carried on without rancour and with a certain kind of love which filled the cracks that appeared between them.

When my brother tried to be a better father than his had been, he thought it would be by making increasing amounts of money for his children to spend and buying them presents. It didn't work. He cannot understand why.

Actually, among the only three genuine presents Papa bought me was an amazing second-hand collection of stories for children called *Uncle Arthur's Cautionary Tales*. They were full of Christianity and horrifying punishments that God meted out to children who displayed any originality or rebelliousness. Good children – who also seemed to die in great numbers – were always shown flying up to heaven, which was all sunlight yellow. It was not at all easy to work out what was good and what was bad and why there was always such a mismatch between the misdemeanours and punishments. I am sure that I read about a little girl called Sarah, who didn't help to wash up and so was punished by the death of her mother. Or maybe I invented that one in my own terrified head.

But, somehow through all the chaos, an innocence had prevailed in our family. Hatred had been kept at bay. The day the plane took off carrying Amir, in 1955, our lives slowly began to putrefy. Something vital had been gouged out. Other certainties began to evaporate too as the empire began to shake and shudder. Nothing was ever to be the same again.

2

When we came back from the airport, Ma, our next-door neighbour, was waiting, hands on ample hips, eyes ablaze: 'Kassam, you are a fool. UK is *kisrani*, what did it teach you?' she shouted at my father, who usually ignored her but on this occasion lashed out and called her a stupid woman. Ma was the most frighteningly powerful woman in the neighbourhood. She would have flattened him with one blow had my mother not stood between them. Papa went into the house muttering as he often did and left us all to weep in peace.

Japan refused to eat for days and would not polish my father's shoes – something he was obsessional about – for weeks.

But it was my mother's anguish I remember the most. Her joy revolved around cooking my brother's favourite food and watching him devour it even if it was two o'clock in the morning. At the age of seventy-four, it still is. After Amir had left, I often found her sitting alone in the kitchen, in the dusk, quietly crying for him. We could only afford to have one light on in the house so dark spots to hide your grief were not hard to find. Her precious son hardly wrote, so she had to reread letters for weeks in order to survive the pain. Amir's process of hardening his heart had already begun. Later, when he found it hard to accept that I was becoming a woman and his anger would blast out of him, my mother would plead with him and God for a return to those days when he cared. I think he still cares, deeply, but he cannot excavate those feelings without destroying them, buried as they now are under so much rubble, so much bitterness.

Anyway, after Babu left I spent as much time as I could out in the corridor or with the other neighbours, all of whom seemed to have a tenderness that we had lost. The house seemed sadder than it had ever been and suddenly I could see the real reason for my mother's deep unhappiness. I also understood why I was still made to sleep between my mother and my father.

The only thing that consoled my mother through her grief was her passionate belief in education and the faith that her son would indeed get the best of that in England. Everything was of course the best in England. She was obsessed with education because she realised that, without money, it would be the only way her children could climb out of their debilitating existence. It was also a way of gaining supremacy.

She knew that the fact that her three children shone at school overturned the hierarchy carefully arranged by this strange dislodged community. 'Money doesn't stop them raising fools and idiots,' Mother would unkindly mutter in Gujarati, especially when she ended up teaching those who were considered too slow to attend the most basic classes in school. But the prizes at the Aga Khan School still went to the children of those who handed out the biggest donations. The final straw came after I had to take over from the weeping Parin (she came to school in a shiny black car with her sister who wore stockings), who couldn't even get to the second verse of 'Where Are You Going To, My Pretty Maid?' before dashing stupidly off the stage. She still won the prize and my proud mother decided enough was enough and put me into an ordinary, downmarket, Asian school which had fewer resources but less injustice too. In later years we used to mock the pupils at the Aga Khan School because they were so pretentious and uncomfortable in their green blazers and woollen socks. Then, at seventeen, I fell in love with one of them – a handsome chap who thought he could sing 'It's Been a Hard

Day's Night', and I wished more than the whole world that I too could wear those uppity blazers instead of the grey home-made cotton skirts and blouses that made up our uniform.

The best thing about the new school was that Japan used to walk me there and back, letting me buy and eat peanuts and raw mangoes along the way and not worrying too much about whether we were late. He had acquired a special position in our family and he knew it. I think that is why he refused to be drawn away by the tempting wages offered to him by our rich folk who loved the food he cooked for their weddings.

He was called John when he came to us. Servants in Kampala invariably ended up being called John, Peter, Paul or Mary because employers could not be bothered to learn their African names. Those who rebelled against this chose their own alternative names. I knew a Chastity, an Immaculate, two sisters who called themselves Sunlight and Moonlight, and Shillingi, the gardener at my primary school who adored money. Japan got his name from a popular Hindi song which he could sing perfectly and of which he never tired. For a while he thought he would call himself Johnnie Walker after a popular comic star in Hindi films, who had apparently himself got the name from his favourite whisky. But he changed his mind because he knew that would enable people to make him into a John. The song, 'Mera Jutta Hai Japani, ye Patloon Englishtani, Sur pe lal topi Russi, Phir bhi dil hai Hindustani' ('My shoes are Japanese, my trousers are English, the red cap I wear is Russian but my heart is Indian') might have been banned by the British in India had they understood the implications. Instead not only was the whole of urban Africa singing it, but Kasookoo too, the parrot who belonged to Ma next door, whose screeches drove us madder than we already were.

Japan's cheerful disposition couldn't hide the reality of his life, though I guess it made it slightly more tolerable. And he always had his dignity. I hated the sight of his naked black feet and the torn shirts he lovingly washed on Sundays and hung out to dry while he rubbed damp soap on his skin till it shone like the waxed floor in our house. They could never explain to me why it had to be that way.

My father despised sentimentality, so carefully had he modelled himself on the tight-lipped Englishman. He found the sorrow in the house intensely irritating, and my mother's tears most of all. I never cried in front of Papa – there is not much point when you know, and I knew at a very young age, that they would not achieve the effect that tears are meant to. Was I afraid of him? No. I just found his indifference and emotional indolence puzzling and occasionally infuriating. Maybe he wasn't indifferent. I once found a tattered copy of a newspaper photo of me deep in his inside pocket. I was digging for cash like my mother had asked me to do. It was me receiving a prize for winning an elocution competition from some bald, important-looking white chap. She said this showed he loved me. I knew it was because he wanted to show off to his drunken friends in the City Bar that he had a clever daughter. Nothing to do with love. Everything to do with conceit. A father's love was conspicuously missing in our relationship and when I was a woman it was then much too easy to elevate any man who cuddled me or smiled lovingly at a child.

City Bar was a popular bar where boastful Asian men gathered. It was where my father sat for days on end in the first years of his married life, drinking and gambling away my mother's meagre dowry. She said she didn't mind that. But when he took Babu and Didi and left them in the car until three in the morning and drove her mad with worry, my mother did what no women ever did. She walked over with Japan and accosted Papa at City Bar. He twisted her finger then till it broke. It was in front of his friends, who roared with drunken laughter and it was the only time in his life my father was violent. That broken finger cured him of gambling, though.

He always forgot everything that mattered. How can you do so much damage with so little malice?

Then there was the day he forgot to pick me up from school and they locked me in for seven hours until the large lady nurse came to open the school up as the evening dispensary. Fat and placid I was then; I put two chairs together and went to sleep. Only cried when they started to show pity. Fatma Nurse, as big as the door, shouting sympathetically in my ear about my poor mother and her eternal suffering and that no good man my father, with his brains lost among the pages of a book. She crushed my nose into her chest and rocked me without caring. But there must have been some good times.

It was wearing to have your father constantly described as a very clever man but a fool when it came to the practical things of life. Once recently, friends I had not seen for many years turned up from Canada and sure enough before the evening was out we were falling about laughing at that story when Kassam forgot where he had parked his car near the City Bar and how he ended up reporting it stolen only to be charged with wasting police time when they found it where he had left it.

Bit by bit my mother started telling me these stories as her sorrow turned to deep melancholy during the months that followed my brother's departure. How she was orphaned and she had to live, first in Tanzania and then Uganda, with her gentle and considerate brother, Sachu, who found himself entangled in some dubious transactions — a weakness that seems to have passed down to many of his children who, one by one, fall inadvertently into some misdemeanour and have to find slightly crooked ways out of the crisis. You always know this is happening when they are no longer to be found in the house, town or sometimes even the country they once inhabited.

Sachu Mama was a genuinely good man who, in trying to make ends meet, took a few ethical short cuts, and in the process met up with my father newly arrived from England with a hat and all the impressive but empty snobbery and big talk of an imitation Englishman. Somehow, my mother exchanged hands as part of some complicated arrangement.

She was whisked off after a civil marriage to make her life at sixteen with a man she did not know, seventeen years older than her and who thought that he was getting some kind of cherub bride to mould at will. Why did she agree? I asked her. 'I was a young girl, with no parents. My brother loved me deeply. He had been so good to me, he had so many children to feed. What right did I have to disagree?'

The wedding night was catastrophic. My mother didn't know what to do and my father was not patient enough to show her. On a damp mattress, her fate was sealed and it was a fate she never shirked.

She still protects his memory, saying she understands how irritating her naivety must have been for him after years in Paris and London. But he had married her for that, her purity. Somehow he could never decide whether he wanted us all to be sophisticated or innocent. I do know, though, that he spent hours with Aunty, a Parsee lady who wore skin-tight bodice blouses and knew all about sundowners and whisky glasses. She treated him with contempt, which charmed him.

Mummy became best friends with Aunty. Together, long after the death of my father, they sit and discuss his wayward ways with a shared fondness which is quite baffling.

These days, when my friends visit, my mother captures them like the Ancient Mariner and recounts many of these stories. She laughs much more than they do when she tells them. Laughs straight from the belly, as one does when life has been so hard that battle is the only thing you know: 'He took me to the film in the first week after we were married. So absent-minded just went out to buy cigarettes and forgot me. I am sixteen, alone and all those Africans outside. I asked this woman to take me home and he was snoring in his bed. So I never went to the films with him again. But you know, he was not a bad man. Only not so reliable. And it was just my *nasib*, my fate. But you know, he never stopped me. He gave me my freedom to do things, I made my life. I could go to the music parties, cinema. I had so many friends. Even now, I can go around

America all alone, I don't worry about that. I have friends. So he didn't look after us, but I learned to take care of myself. He never ordered me to do anything. Only the frocks. He did not like me to wear frocks, when everyone started these things. No, in that he was stubborn. Only saris he liked me to wear.'

For my mother, this was a subtle sign of how much he really cared about her. A man telling you what you could wear or not somehow reasserted the power balance as it should be, as it wasn't in our home. Sometimes less changes than you hope or think. I was astonished when a childhood friend who goes in for power dressing and jobs in the City told me, eyes shining with pride, how she was so loved, how her husband would never let her show her arms in public and how he had asked her to cover her nipples with a Band-Aid when she was wearing a blouse which was slightly transparent. Ownership is love.

Once Papa set fire to himself, Japan told me, by putting a lit cigarette into his pyjama pocket. Another time when the debtors came looking for him he hid in a dustbin which Japan had to sit on and whistle while they searched for him high and low, making my mother cry as they accused her of hiding him. Ratan, the panwallah, who was across the street saw it all and told the story to all his customers, adding to the constant humiliation that we felt.

The stories I always wanted my mother to tell me were the ones I least understood. Papa had this curious habit of disappearing. One day, just like that. Out to buy cigarettes, seen again after three or four years usually after a begging letter in which he asked my mother to forgive him and to borrow money for his return fare from the chachas and mamas or, if they didn't oblige (and they didn't after the first time), from Chaturbhai, the round-faced, beaming, kind man downstairs who owned the shirt shop. Most people by then knew the hard and unpredictable life my mother had to lead and although they would resent it, help would usually be forthcoming. They knew she was proud enough to pay them back even if it took years and we had to have dhal three times a week. Sometimes people would be spontaneously generous and that really hurt. Mr Patel of the stationery shop would smile protectively when I went into his shop, pat my oiled head and then (after carefully wiping his greasy hand) pick out a free pencil or eraser. On a bad day, of course, he would turn brusque, assuming I had come in to beg for more, when all I ever wanted was to spend my ten cents on something I wanted.

Where did Papa go during all those lost years? He always ended up in England. I used to imagine that he had a glamorous secret life over there. Maybe he was part of the underground movement of students fighting for Indian independence. Maybe there was another family there, as abandoned as we were. Was there a siren? How can I easily forgive him for disappearing before I was born? Especially when, they tell me, on his return, when I was a year old, instead of coming home he went to see Aunty, who told him to go home to see his bonny baby. Thank God I looked like him, otherwise people would have given up on my mother altogether.

My mother became skilful at managing. At charming the rationwallah who was waiting to be paid. At making sure that whatever it took, we would be dressed in new clothes and underwear on our birthdays. At making clothes for the carpenter's family in exchange for a cupboard or a bed. At never feeling sorry for herself when she went to the cinema on her own or when at weddings, she would be invited alone. Or always begging for lifts because that's the only way she could go out at night, and then putting up with the surly faces of those who would oblige but increasingly found it burdensome. Or having friends who had a lot more money than us (even millionaires in their chauffeur-driven cars), and making it an event in their lives when, after going to the market, they could come in for a chat and some of my mother's special tea and bhajias. She taught me how not to feel ashamed of having less than others and how to teach them that we were as good as they were. To this day, in her tiny council flat, visitors arrive in their massive cars from all over the world. Talking for an hour to

24

Jena is an essential part of their packed schedule. If they fail, one day, she will make them feel awful about it as only she can.

Funny being so young and being so aware of the tragedy and the comedy at the same time of our lives. Funny too, how many skills you can pick up from your parents. For years, every Saturday, my rich friend took me to see films, often a Chaplin or Laurel and Hardy followed by a loud and merciless western in which we cheered the white cowboys. Her mother would pay and declare her gratitude because her daughter was with such a polite and clever little child.

Living so near the marketplace was not always great. I hated the screams of the chickens when their throats were being cut, and I hated them even more when I went to the market with my mother and she chose the bird which had to die in front of our tightly closed eyes. But most hateful of all was the terrible cry which would set off when some poor petty African thief was spotted, and this would happen regularly. One cry would be overlaid by another until it became an ululation, partly vengeful and partly already mourning the young man the crowd was out to get. Only a beating if he was lucky or if it was too hot and the crowd was tired. Death, otherwise. A daring young life for a bunch of onions or a loaf of bread. I would hide under the bed with pillows over my ears until the wailing stopped. Then I would look out and many times there would be a bloody body, burning sometimes on the footpath outside the made-in-England shirt shop where the highly desirable boxed polyester shirts (a sign of how much more sophisticated you were compared to those dressed merely in cotton shirts made by half-blind tailors even though you began to smell like rotting cheese in the warm weather within hours) were stacked up in the window together with striped ties and dead flies. Chaturbhai, the owner, would curse and moan about bad omens for business while the poor wretch awaited removal. My mother, who hated this as much as I did, once hid a thief who ran up the corridor to escape the crowds chasing him.

Then she stood, all four foot ten inches of her and confronted representatives of the sweating, throbbing crowd, denying all knowledge of the man. The following month he came and gave her a bunch of bananas for her troubles, but three shirts mysteriously vanished from the washing line that day.

Those days, I often used to go next door and weep on Ma's lap, tears slipping and sliding off the shiny synthetic clothes she always wore – she too believing as we all did that nylon, and later polyester and Terylene, was superior to the local cotton. And if you were really a somebody, you had greater aspirations. You would probably drink cocoa at night and wear Clark's shoes. These were the crumbs of England that dropped around us and which we fell upon with unseemly, unthinking eagerness. They gave us illusions that we too were civilised and worth something.

Years later, Bha, the father of the man who was to be my first husband, a cobbler who made ugly golden sandals for brides and women he liked, used to boast that they were just like Clark's shoes. As I tottered around in these sandals, one not quite as high as the other and both precariously unbalanced, through endless twisted ankles and forced smiles I would listen to him going on 'I was a master of shoes, *beta*, even the English ladies came in to buy my shoes.' Then would follow the story we had heard a thousand times before, how the Aga Khan and his brother, sent to East Africa during the war when they were boys, came to his shop and how he served them samosas and how once an English judge came in to have his shoes repaired. When Bha became mentally ill after leaving Uganda, and began to starve himself to death, in the years that followed our expulsion by Idi Amin, these were the only stories that still gave him joy, a sense of what he had once been, a pompous man who knew he was always right 'and the best'. But I loved him.

3

I also loved that other mountain of cruelty and arrogance, Ma. She was not related to us, but she was the only granny I knew. She was a big woman with yards of creamy skin and copious redundant flesh which moved around and bulged in different places depending on what she was wearing and what she was doing. Not that she actually did very much. A deeply religious Sunni Muslim, she sat on her leather seat, *tasbi* in hand, next to the balcony from where she observed the street and commanded her household. Her arms flopped menacingly as she waved them around, commenting on the harlots who were walking along the road – anyone who wore a short dress, particularly with a stiff underskirt, to Ma was a harlot – and screaming out orders to her servants and her family. This consisted in the early days of three grown-up sons, and a daughter, all physically completely different from each other, because each was a product of a different father whom Ma had disposed of as she travelled across from Mombasa where she had arrived as a little girl from India and been married off to her first husband, a man much older than herself and good and kind, she said.

Those were precarious times for the pioneers who had arrived from the Indian subcontinent to open up the interior of East Africa. Many died along the way. Some were explorers who risked life and limb to go into areas where no outsiders had

27

ever been and settled in the middle of villages. The street where we lived was named after the greatest of these pioneers – Allidina Visram. A man who set up a whole network of shops from the coast to the heart of the interior, a legend that remained barely recognised by us when we went to school where we were inevitably taught the brave story of the intrepid Livingstone and Speke. Alibhai, Ma's first husband, was a railway worker 'with so many wounds', she would proudly remember. He was the one she really loved of the four men she ended up marrying. Perhaps because he died before she had grown to detest him. 'Died slowly of blood poisoning after he stepped on some broken glass on the railway line,' she would repeat to herself, whenever she thought of him. There were no medical facilities for these workers.

She started smoking his cigarettes after he died, a young bride of eighteen, alone and planning her survival amongst relatives she did not trust and who were intent on blaming her for his death – 'She brought the curse, with those strange grey-green eyes' – and on ousting her before she made any claims on them.

Ma, who was once regarded as a great beauty because of those eyes and her fair skin, then had three more husbands, each discarded when they outlived their usefulness and hardly ever mentioned by the time she had settled down in Kampala, with all her children. The husbands were clearly still besotted with her because they kept her supplied with money, clothes, and the most devoted, a successful grocer in Mombasa, all her dry grocery needs, including foul-smelling dried prawns. The more romantic ex-husband sent her boxes full of silky, satiny fabrics, and chiffon scarves for her head sprinkled with *oudh*, a dense, sweet, sexy Arabic perfume which lingered in the household for days. She never saw them herself although the boys were sent across occasionally, usually when they needed money. My mother, who had to fend for herself and all of us in spite of a husband in tow, could not understand this. Perhaps Ma left before the hunger of a man for her had been satisfied, keeping him addicted to hope, always her slave, needing to prove to himself that he was not worthless. They were all referred to as *sala soover* – 'bloody pigs'. When she was cross with the offspring, they would become the children of these pigs. And when the two sons got married bringing with them fragile beautiful women whose parents had virtually given them away because they would have a chance to go to East Africa, they too were the *soovers* or *kuthis* – bitches.

Almira, the elder one, died in 1994 in her small, damp house in Bolton. The years of cruelty that had been inflicted on her by Ma had made her a bitter, screeching woman. But I remembered her and Zubine when they had arrived. Gentle, sweet and kind, they were completely unprepared for the physical and emotional severity of the house they had arrived into.

Ma's cigarettes were kept locked in a drawer, together with all her other loot, including the money her boys earned as garage mechanics. They were abject creatures, spineless, afraid, weak and threatening in a pent-up sort of way. Long before I became aware of it, the eldest one, Moosa, had made his escape by making his mother disown him. He did this by marrying a woman who was not a Sunni Muslim and who wore lipstick and rouge and dresses that revealed her enormous ankles and feet. She had five gold teeth which flashed ominously when she smiled. Shari made it her business to visit Ma regularly as an act of provocation. She was utterly immune to the insults and abuse she faced and would force her many children to sit on the lap of their grandmother, who regarded them as contaminated creatures from another planet. 'Go *beta*, sit on Ma, don't be afraid, she will give you a sweetie.' Often, Shari would place the wailing child on Ma's lap. Within seconds, the child would slip off the reluctant lap and fall on the floor and cry real tears only to be smacked by Ma for making too much noise.

Banu, the only daughter, was different from her half-brothers. She was dark skinned, and would have been blighted had it not been for the fact that she had inherited her mother's astonishing power and was never easy to dominate the way her brothers were. In the Asian community, of course, to be attractive you had to be fair skinned, have a 'nice and pretty wheaten complexion'. To be irresistible, light eyes were what you needed. 'She is so lovely,' my mother still eulogises, whenever she sees a cream-coloured Asian woman. 'You'd think she is a *dholki* (white woman). You can see the water going down her white throat when she drinks.' An exquisitely beautiful (dark) South Indian friend of mine was once pronounced by her to be a *bichari* (poor thing). 'Who will marry her?' When she later met her handsome doctor husband, my mother decided he was a heroically compassionate man: 'Look, you see, there are men like this also. God looks after us all.'

Although she was never allowed to use makeup, Ma did permit Banu to splash her dark face with white talcum powder, so that she didn't look as dark as the Africans. My mother advised her to stop drinking tea and coffee because she was convinced the dye seeped through and darkened the skin. I drank my first cup of tea when I was eighteen, an act of defiance that still incenses my mother. As soon as she could, Banu surprised us all by finding herself Latif, a very pale-skinned man with pink cheeks and a dear innocence which she exploited all their happy lives together. She loved cheap and loud hairclips in bright metallic colours with multicoloured glass stones. They would be shaped like bows, flowers, birds, butterflies and English cottages with roses winding up them. These, she stuck on her hair to keep up the curious mounds and twists she created on top of her head. Sometimes it was two little horns on either side of the top of her head, sometimes thick plaits wound like a halo or, the most outrageous, her hair left open and pinned back on either side. I was quite stunned to see that now, when she is a grandmother of seven, she has started wearing a *hijab* to cover her hair and worrying about male lasciviousness. Her daughter, the once hapless Khatun, who is now as formidable and large as her grandmother once was, thinks her mother is mad. 'Is anyone dead, that you are dressing in these clothes?' she demands as she waddles past in her richly embroidered *shalwar khamizes* shimmering with gold even on a boring old rainy Tuesday in Bolton.

Although Banu was independent then, she never had the courage to break free from her mother. After she got married, Ma made sure that she stayed on as part of the household, going off every evening to a rented bedroom nearby with her husband and ever-increasing brood and reappearing the next morning to make the tea. Latifbhai had to cope with that greatest insult a man could face: he was a *ghar jamai*, a man who lived with his in-laws (the rented room didn't count because it was used only as a bed), a wimp, a puppet, to be scorned and mocked. 'Where is your thing, yaar,' they would shout at him from the pan shop. 'Has she cut it off? or has her mother locked it in her drawer?' He took it all with such a lovely smile that in the end he won even his own embarrassed parents over. 'It' had clearly not gone anywhere and was performing with admirable efficiency if the number of children – eight in all, over ten years – his wife produced were of his making.

With each childbirth Banu grew wider and more like her mother, sometimes even behaving alarmingly like her. She was never cruel, though. Not like Ma, whose sadistic impulses especially towards those she had weakened was unwatchable. She terrorised the household and the neighbourhood. Even the market traders, who called her 'Mamkuba' – Big Mother – and whom she abused constantly, would bring their best fare to her in the mornings before setting up their stalls. They feared her as some demonic creature from an African myth who needed to be pacified in order for the rains to fall and the food to grow.

They also knew that occasionally and unpredictably she would have a flash of generosity and they would get an unimaginably large baksheesh which would make all the degradation worth while.

But Ma loved my mother, I think because she identified another woman whose life was messed up by the thoughtlessness of men – which incomprehensibly was how she thought of her own life – but more importantly, because my mother had defined herself and made her own space and this made her special. She also spoilt me and I loved her for it. She thought I was sharp and therefore deserved special treatment, so we had secrets. She would open the drawer, which she could hide with her enormous girth, and as she bent over to get her cigarette out of the Players packet, she would look at me with her grey, conspiratorial eyes and put something into my palm. I knew I had to wait until I was out of the house before I could see whether it was money wrapped in newspaper – something she did each month when her sons handed over their wages – or chocolate which would melt in seconds, and that made me very anxious, but I knew even then that one did not scurry away from despots, even for precious Cadbury's plain milk choco-late, until one was properly dismissed. After every exam, the gifts were more substantial. These she did not hide from her family but used to humiliate her granddaughter Khatun, who was the same age as me but who always failed all her exams, except cookery and needlework. I cared so little about the tears that were shed by Khatun, it makes me ashamed. But I was young and selfish and the adoration I felt for this remarkable woman was left untouched even by the screams of the servants (and later the daughters–in–law) who were being viciously beaten by her for some (often fabricated) misdemeanour, or when she personally slaughtered the goat she had been fattening, positively relishing the bloody ritual.

The bathroom where the deed was done stank for days and the red footsteps on the cement floor used to make me want to throw up in memory of the goat which all of us children had grown to like. I also refused to eat any of the goat curry from the huge vat that simmered on an open fire outside the flat. The smell got into our hair and bodies and it reminded us of the horror. But this is when Ma became her most generous, giving the cooked goat to anyone who came to the door and even allowing (for a change) Johnnie, her long-suffering servant, a couple of proper meals.

Religion provided respite for Ma's victims especially when at the time of Abraham's sacrifice, the hajj, the atmosphere of redemption was about. This is why she slaughtered the goats and spoke in a soft voice. The times to be good were taken very seriously indeed and there was a fear of God almost tangibly around. They weren't merely hypocritical gestures. Something profound did happen to people like Ma. It just didn't last. It was as if this was a time to fuel up with piety. When others tried the same trick, Ma was disdainful. When some Shia Muslim groups flagellated themselves with small chains and flick knives for a month during Mohorrum: 'They think Allah is a fool? None of this blood will wash their sins, the dogs. Then they go and eat biriyani in the *mascheed*.'

The only thing that I found irksome about Ma was her demand every evening that the children, and especially me, should walk all over her for half an hour as she lay down on a huge cotton mattress. This was her relaxation, and three of us would have to do this without falling off her flaccid flesh, which felt as if it would roll off and make huge fatty puddles around us. As we pounded on it, she sweated freely and our feet would get wet and warm. If we giggled we would be in trouble, especially Khatun, who would get a beating.

The only other person she treated with complete compassion and care was Georgie, the beggar with elephantiasis, who struggled up slowly every week and waited patiently, laughing at his own observations while Ma gave him food, lovingly dished out by herself, and money to spend. His legs were enormous, with skin that was dry, wrinkled, unfeeling. Various insects had made their home in the deep crevices of these astonishing legs – some were brazen enough to fly out when he was standing patiently outside the door – and the open wounds were a favourite haunt. He could only shuffle a few inches at a time and this meant that he was frequently abused for being always in the way or teased mercilessly by children playing around him. This did not deter the man from shining forth in his most pleasant manner and beaming at everyone. Come to think of it, beaming and smiling – which I was very good at too – was the only way to get round Ma. Weeping and wailing only made her want more of the same. This was a lesson the other *maskinis* had not learned. They usually fared badly when they approached Ma, except on a Friday, which, being a holy day, saw Ma on her best behaviour as Allah was watching.

As time went on Ma began to believe with increasing zeal that she could get away with anything because she was so utterly faithful to the Book. *Namaaz* five times a day, a scrupulous following of all the rules and a genuine belief that if she did all this she could carry on appallingly, Monday to Thursday and weekends too, and between her and God they would reach an agreement about retribution.

In Ma's house there was a row of bedrolls piled up along the long corridor. The bedroom contained an enormous dining table where people would eat. Then the table would be dismantled into three separate bits and be moved into the veranda, so that the bedding could be laid on the floor. The occupancy changed as marriages took place and children began to arrive. The couples would sleep in rented rooms nearby which they could go to only after Ma had extracted every ounce of energy and joy out of them and if they did not appear at six o'clock the following morning the mutterings and taunts would begin. To the sons: 'You have become slaves to your wives now. Show your manhood. Lying in the arms of a woman until now. You are pathetic.' To the wives: 'I know about black magic, that is what you have done. But Allah is greater than your magic. My boys are my boys.' Nobody would say anything in response because they were mortified by the sexual references. The boys eventually got used to being made to feel guilty and dirty for sleeping with their wives and the women for being witches and *kuthis* for encouraging such a thing in her innocent sons.

Banu was exempted from this abuse and she carried on blossoming and procreating happily, ignoring totally the wretched lives of her sisters-in-law. When Zubine failed to produce children and Almira did not deliver as regularly as she was expected to, Ma would call them barren whores. It was Zubine's fertile replacement who had the last laugh at Ma's deathbed. When Shabnab arrived, haughty and irritated that the house she had been brought into was no bigger than the cowshed (she said) she had left behind in the newly formed Pakistan, power in the family began inexorably to shift.

Zubine hated her more than she hated Ma and decided that she would spend her time exploiting the animosity between the two women.

She spent most of her time after that in the kitchen, still remembering when and what Ma liked to eat and drink and serving it with a bitter sweetness, managing somehow not to let her sense of failure cloud her sweet, warm personality. The radio in the kitchen kept her company. Intensely sad Hindi songs about duty, love and motherhood were her favourites. She also loved plastic and feather flowers, which she placed lovingly in small tins around the house.

Ma usually spoke in imperatives. She expected to be pleased and never to show that she was pleased. And her biggest indulgences were played out with food, which she loved with great gusto but about which she was inhumanly precise. It had to be made exactly as she commanded. At every stage the saucepan had to be brought across to her to comment on. It was never good enough even then. It was only for Eid, when she herself got off her throne, that one actually got to taste her cooking. It was truly unforgettable, though unnecessarily ostentatious with pools of ghee swimming at the top and almonds and pistachios covering the vermicelli.

The last time I saw her was in May 1972. She was lying in bed, curled up to half her size, convinced that her new daughter-in-law had poisoned her and cursing her wildly in a soft grating voice, feeling sorry for herself that she had no cigarettes (they had finally wrenched the key from her and found piles of money and cigarettes) and, worst of all, no gold anywhere on her hands and arms. I put one of my rings on her finger and wept with her, hating all those who had reduced that massive creature to this wreck. Her sons looked unconcerned, enjoying thoroughly their moment of triumph over their mother whose domination had paralysed them for so long. Shabnam, brought in because Zubine had failed to produce any children, treated the old woman with blasphemous contempt. I left Kampala the next day, part of the exodus of Asians already making their departure from Uganda, and she died a few days later.

The impulse to believe in the goodness of adults is so overwhelming when you are a child that it blinds you. Without Ma, though, we might not have survived the worst times that our family was to go through when the rot really began to set in. There was no reason why she should have supported us at all. After all she was a Sunni Muslim and we were Shia Ismailis, sworn enemies according to fiery missionaries who periodically arrived in Uganda from the subcontinent to tell us how it was or should be. The bitter religious and political enmities that were exploding all over India and Pakistan meant little to any of us. At least within the discrete Asian community the barriers were breaking down. Pity we could not extend ourselves more to the African.

4

Our block had four flats along an open corridor which overlooked the market. Each had a sitting room, which we all seemed to paint a terrible bright green colour (it was cheaper to buy three big pots of paint than one and three pots, if we were frugal and painted around the pictures and calendars, would do all the flats) and a bedroom. There was a long balcony at the front where we sat in the evening after we'd had our baths, watching the changing light and the bustle of the streets dying down before Ratan opened up his pan shop and the bars downstairs started buzzing. We would shout across to each other the tiny bits of information about the day the others might miraculously have missed. With all the doors always open, sharp eyes on the lookout and the innocence of observant children, there were no secrets in that block.

Maybe that is why, as time went on, Mr Desai, a tall, bald, imposing man from house No. 3, took a vow of silence, so that no rows were ever heard between him and his family and we were all truly astonished when his very traditional wife took off with two of her daughters and returned to India, never to be seen again. Why, remains a mystery to this day, even to the many other daughters and sons she left behind. How did six daughters, two sons and parents fit into a two-roomed flat, and how indeed had it been possible to add to the brood at such regular intervals? And why had Shantaben never told them she was leaving? These questions were discussed quietly by the neighbours, who found the family's privacy intensely irritating.

Our kitchen was dark and initially had a Primus stove and some sparse utensils arranged neatly on a shelf. On another shelf, rows of jars held rice, lentils, dried beans and spices. There was a small meat safe with wire gauze where my mother stored fresh food. She used to stitch up the tears in the gauze with embroidery thread and a needle. Her soft hands – still so very soft and small – would bleed for days after that so I had to do the hemming on the sari blouses she made for the women in the mosque. At seven, the pride I felt when praised for my invisible hemming outweighed any boredom and discomfort.

As time went on, the other neighbours acquired a fridge. We only had a *matoongi*, a clay water pot with a beautiful brass cover, stand and serving cup. The water was always cool, but in our house it smelt of Brasso because my houseproud mother insisted on polishing the serving cup every week. Next to the kitchen was the bathroom, which consisted of a wet floor and tap and a squat toilet, one step up. When we were nine, my chubby cherubic friend Shireen and I were caught sitting on this step revealing to each other what lay under our knickers. It caused a major scandal and endless jokes among the other kids in the block. But it was a big moment of freedom for me and I did not regret it.

I had always been ashamed of the coarse dark blue cotton knickers my mother made for me out of my sister's old school uniforms. They had elastic at the top and round the legs so they bulged and they itched. I had never shown them to anybody. Now, with our explorations, I had seen that it did not matter what you wore as underwear. It's what you are inside that matters. Shireen had these posh nylon knickers with pink and white frills rippling right across. It made no difference to her wobbly thighs. I have never bought fancy knickers in my entire life.

Besides us and Ma and the Desais, with their silent father and umpteen children, we had the Patels who were posh and refined and who had the money and the hearts to bail out any of us when the need arose. Their sitting room was painted pink. Ramankaka Patel came to get my mother out of hospital when I was born. She had no cash to pay the hospital bill and without that she was not allowed to discharge herself.

We missed them when they eventually moved to their vast house in Kololo with a thousand roses and brutal Alsatian dogs who never let you wander around the beautiful gardens in peace.

Sometimes I feel terribly guilty that I had to arrive and add to the burdens already bearing down too heavily on my mother. The misery of having a neighbour pick us up to come home from hospital, of not knowing where Papa was and trying not to hate him because being upset would be bad for the baby. The struggles that Babu and Didi went through, carrying tea and toast to her in hospital in a teapot, with a teacosy, their little hands burning. The fears she must have had about another little mouth to feed, ten years after the last one. To be so thin and ill that when I was born I weighed only three and a half pounds, like a medium-sized aubergine, she said. It was not surprising that she could produce no breast milk and then soon afterwards collapsed with meningitis.

But although she tells me the story of my inauspicious birth, I know that my arrival gave her a new burst of energy to take on the world. It is the way she talks with such exhilaration about how quickly she made me into a podgy baby, replete with expensive Cow & Gate milk which created even greater debts. No wonder I couldn't walk until the age of two. I remember the pink taffeta costume she made me when I was the queen eating bread and honey for the celebrations at the mosque. Or how she walked to my school every few months and interrogated the teachers about what they were teaching me. How constantly she told me that everybody loved me because I was so contented, placid and clever: 'She was so good, you know, we couldn't find her in the house because she had fallen asleep under the table, bed or in the balcony.'

At lunchtime the least clumsy children of each household would be asked to carry over whatever had been cooked for that day to the other three flats. There was of course undeclared competition between the women. Ma abstained from this ritual because it equalised her more than she found comfortable. So she would receive without gratitude and, like a queen, bestow her food upon us from time to time at odd hours when it was least expected.

She sometimes felt beleaguered and contaminated living among infidels and although this did not infect the way she related to anyone, it came out of a feeling deep in her heart that she and hers were the chosen ones. The Ismailis she despised more than the Hindus because, as Muslims, they should have known better. We belonged to a group which claimed to be Islamic but which she felt went around subverting even the most basic tenets of Islam.

In some ways she was right. We were indeed a strange lot. We had roots in Iran, cultural baggage from India, rituals that had more in common with those sources than the pure Islam that Ma believed in. Mummy would wink at me when Ma pronounced that we would go to hell for this reason or the other. One that made no sense at all – a bit like Uncle Arthur's stories, really – was the warning she gave me about leaving out my little finger when I was stuffing food into my mouth. The finger, she said, would question me in hell. Now this was one she had clearly invented. Hell would be a busy place indeed if fingers were given rights. Ma also thought that, compared to us, she had a proper family life and in an odd sort of way she was right.

My mother tried to do her best, spreading herself to protect and nurture us, but even she was not strong enough to give us the solid, indestructible core that she believed other families in our community had. At the age of seventy-four, she still talks of how she hopes the family will unite before she dies. Her hopes depress me. And I cry too that it took me so long to understand what she had to do to keep us together and bond just a little.

I remember how easily enchanted I was when I met my ex-husband's family. I never saw how they were embittered too, in different ways. All I saw and loved was the fact that fifteen of them, from the great-grandmother down to the grandchildren, would appear at lunchtime. Eight of them lived together in the same small house. The rest came in to eat every day.

Everyone would be speaking at the same time, mostly accusing each other of this and that – 'You have eaten my money, you *sala*', 'Where is the three hundred shillings for the car?' – or being placated by their truly virtuous mother; one complaining that the food was too hot for him to eat quickly and have a nap before returning to work, another shouting that the meat had gone cold. The dotage of their mother did make all the boys (except one) think that their wives would also always succumb to their whims. Fortunately they didn't, but even that was not enough to break the knots that tied this family together. They could be bitingly rude to one another, deeply jealous and ready to malign, but they were, and still are, always solidly together.

On Fridays they would all arrive in mosque, *en masse*, and wherever they chose to stand and talk, the others would never be very far away. They weren't rich but were extremely popular because the men were all so handsome with their creamy skin and chiselled noses and because everyone knew how superhumanly self-effacing their mother was, managing to live with a man whose boorishness was legendary. A real woman. She was also exquisitely beautiful, with long hair tied into an enormous bun and tastefully chosen saris (most dirt cheap) which would come alive on her. Even when she was in her sixties she was capable of turning heads.

Another saving grace was the fact that they were a properly religious family, not like ours where my mother had to continuously erase or excuse the blasphemy her husband committed outside the mosque. To be poor and faithless made you a fool. To be poor and faithful made you a saint.

I know how confused and unhappy Khatibai was when her

son, my ex-husband, departed to live in Huntingdon with his blonde, dog and newly acquired Englishness. This was her favourite son, the one who used to go to mosque at five every morning and who tried so hard not to be like his father. Her grandson was ten then. And all these years on, the memories of her son have faded, but we do miss her. I will not forget the incredible love she and I shared so that we could do little but cry when we spoke on the phone when she was forced to go to Canada as a refugee and we came to England. Or the food she would make just for me and the way she welcomed me into her family, knowing I was odd and came from people who were odder. I spent so many years loving her, wanting to be like her, an angel. I couldn't keep it up. Not when I was expected to tell my weeping son that his father was a good man – those lies that keep families going. So I fell from grace and found my pride. She cannot of course be expected to understand that, though my mother does, completely.

Here were two women who kept their families (sort of) sane, each in her own way, like so many women in our community who were oppressed by new and hard orthodoxies that had been created to give us a sense of a heritage, substance, morality even, and a social order that those who had first arrived could ignore or discard. When you leave your roots behind you lose ease, and all you feel is that dreadful fear that you lack cultural legitimacy. And men can use the moments of doubt and flux to carve out the world even more to suit their position.

Having a man and his sons making impossible demands on you defined you as a proper woman. Having a man who ignored even his own needs was a much more perplexing and taxing situation, and one that demanded a response of innocence and guile in equal measure, otherwise people would find a way of making you culpable in some way for it. 'It is up to the woman, you know. It is in the hands of the woman. A woman can cure the most evil man, but she must have the heart and the will . . .' Such judgements made mostly by women ensured that nothing as sticky as blame ever landed on our men.

I have seen the way men looked at my mother, partly with pity, partly with a kind of lust because she was different, but more because there was no man to protect her honour. She innocently played the games of flirtation so as not to offend them. After all, she never knew when she would need them. I too am a flirt. And men like me. It is deep in my bones and it gets me things just as it got her things. I am so much like my mother. The only one who is. That helped me survive. Or perhaps the other two with their bitter cigarettes and thoughts paid the price I did not have to because I was too young to know.

5

What is the real story about why and how Papa left Karachi in the twenties? There is some hazy tale that floated about which he neither confirmed nor denied. But it is the best we ever got. Seems he left Karachi at the age of seventeen and stowed away on a ship. They found him when they were mid-sea. Then there is a blank until he appears in Uganda, a pukka sahib, wearing his dapper suit, working for some English company, pretending he was better than the rest of the Asians there. So, I used to think to myself again and again, he got on a ship, and went to London, a young man idealistic, in love with the great civilisations of the world, self-taught and arrogant even then thinking that those around him were lesser creatures than he was and for reasons they were too stupid to understand. Those dark silences about his periods in England I used to imagine were because he was involved in some exciting subversive anti-imperialist plots with other radical students who were in England from undivided India. Maybe his emotional detachment came from that early history. Impossible fantasies. In reality he was too much a loner, too self-centred a person to give himself over even to a cause.

When my mother was married off to my father, the wedding could not happen in a mosque because my father had been excommunicated and anyway he despised our religious leaders.

He refused to apologise; my father never apologised for anything in his life. On his deathbed, though, my mother tells me, he got somewhere near saying sorry.

In some ways he *was* better than many of the people around us. His rejection of the herd mentality, his original mind, his bohemian ways, his admirable disregard for etiquette and social lubrication. In our society, where gossip, ingratiation, hypocrisy and a hidden malevolence greased so many social interactions, my father was completely forthright and uninterested in favours. Though I seem to have inherited the frankness, which does not go down too well either amongst my own people or in southern England, I do not have his indifference to the effect that words have on people.

I only have one picture of my father when he was young and defiant. A photographer recently asked me if he was European. With his dark skin? I asked incredulously. 'It's just the way he is dressed and the look, I suppose,' he stuttered. So all those years when he wanted to belong to this country and ran to it for comfort and confidence, abandoning us all, so many times, it did rub off.

Bit by bit, over the years my mother has relived her own early life. Her mother died when she was three. There are no memories. No pictures, no information. Only an enormous sadness, she says, as she tried to face the world with her older sister and her tiny brother, Pilu, who cried for weeks for their mother. Her father, she says, was a very kind man, but he too died before long. Pilu and she had to go and live with her eldest brother Sachu, who had a family of his own and a generosity which forever left them not in poverty but on the brink of it. Her brother's wife, my *maami*, was a kindly soul with an infinite capacity to absorb into her life the many people who made demands on Sachu. A small woman with a hunched back, she had several children but still took in my mother and her brother, and even when widowed at an early age, never abandoned her conviction that she was born to care for all those who came through her door. My Sachu mama loved her deeply and that, says my mother wistfully, was her reward.

But necessity forced decisions that the family were later to regret.

Fatma Masi, my mother's sister, was married off to a man who had a serious drink problem and therefore not much of a choice of brides in that cautious community. Her life was a misery which she bore with a stoicism that eventually killed her. I remember her living in Mwanza in Tanganyika, a swampy town full of potholes and the howls of hyenas at night, in a small tidy house which had a leaky tin roof, umpteen beds and a dug-out latrine which used to terrify me because I was sure a snake would wind its way up and into me. I learned to piss at record speed in that house and prayed desperately whenever I had one of the frequent bouts of dysentery that one always got in Mwanza. Fatma Masi was so kind and warm to all of us. Her teeth all fell out at an early age and so she could not suck on sugar cane the way she once used to, all day long. So she would buy it for all of us — her many children and Didi, Babu and me. It was her patience that stays with me. A pretty important quality when she used to dig out the worms that had crawled into the flesh of my toes, using a blackened safety pin and turmeric to disinfect it. Her hand would remain steady through my wrigglings and screeches and afterwards, instead of screaming back like my mother would have done, all Fatma Masi did was hug me and give me more sugar cane.

Her husband would make occasional drunken appearances and leave her pregnant each time he came for any length of time. The children all suffered and grew stronger. All except one. All except Noor, meaning light, the eldest; the brightest, they say he was. He 'came first in the school'. He was always reading, peering more and more intently through his ever-thickening glasses. The elders thought it was this mania for the written word that corroded first his eyes and then his brain. One day, he stopped going to the post office where he worked, got into his striped pyjamas and gave up on life. The rest of the family took it in turns to feed him and coax some joy back into him. He just stared back and curled up tighter into his bed. In time he just became part of the way it was, with people talking to him without expecting an answer and feeding him like they would a beloved but ailing dumb animal. They were never irritated with him and took him to weddings whenever the invitation said 'family', with a jacket over his pyjamas and a protective arm across his shoulders.

In many other families, mentally ill people were either seen as representatives of the Devil, who had come to try a family, or as an acute embarrassment. One family tethered their son who was born with cerebral palsy, like a goat, to a ring against a wall in an outhouse. In another building which had several flats, whenever we went visiting we heard the tortured, hoarse cries of a woman they said had been locked up in a room since birth.

Noor remains somewhere in Mwanza, I wish I knew where. The rest of the siblings, scattered around the world, have all made good. But they remain humble, timid even, as if they can never forget the humiliation of living a life which everyone described as even worse than a *gola*'s. *Gola* was the term we used to disparagingly describe the black man, who also had his own contemptuous words to describe us.

Going to Mwanza was one of the joys of our lives. My cousin Mansoor — who would also send us tins of ghee, oil and flour when times were really rough at home — once in a while sent us second-class tickets for the steamer which would take us across Lake Victoria to Mwanza. I remember the deckchairs and . . . and utterly handsome men with set sneers in sparkling uniforms and tiny cabins where we would all huddle and take it in turns to look out of the window. We would usually know the other families also travelling second class and the children knew how to cheat the system so that we could use the first-class facilities without getting caught.

My mother would pack food in a tiffin for three days — though even her food was inedible by the third — and at the other end on a nest of hard jutting rocks would be waiting all twelve cousins yelling, waving their hankies and falling into the water. Unlike my rich Ramzan chacha's house which paralysed me with fear, here there was nothing but a good time to be had on as little money as possible. My *maasi*, my *maami*, and their many children loved us, and especially my mother, their *bai*, with a passion. It was only here that I saw my mother put aside the endless problems of her life, because here she expected to be spoilt.

Anoo was my favourite cousin. A genius with his hands, he would make me beautiful doll's furniture from matchboxes, pieces of wood and silver foil paper collected from cigarette packets. Sometimes he would find gold paper and this made beautiful goblets. The cupboards had pull-out drawers and mirrors. I knew if they were really good my mother would make me some small dolls out of scraps of material. I would watch him for hours sitting outside, getting dustier by the minute and going off to browse in the Christian bookshop nearby whenever I got bored.

Already mad about books, there I would gaze at stapled booklets full of fire and brimstone watched by pious Benjamin, who tried not to look suspicious because that would have been an unchristian and uncharitable thing to do. He shed this mask one terrifying day when a huge monitor lizard, the size of a small crocodile, lazily shuffled into the shop in the heat of the afternoon. He jumped over the counter as we all screamed and shrank into corners, terrified of both the animal and his attacker, who had turned into a wild-eyed monster. Mercilessly he slashed the poor bewildered creature with a panga spouting blood all over the books and the hanging rosaries. The next time I dared to go into the shop, Benjamin was there in his white robe, peace upon his face and not a spot of blood anywhere.

Mwanza was that sort of place. Hardly a real town, where man, woman, beast, bird and insect trod on each other's lives constantly and where it wasn't possible to keep up a civilised distance between you and nature. Dust roads which turned when it rained into gooey mud baths meant that the most polished and expensive car looked like the hand-drawn carts that market traders were pulling beside it. Posh houses were smeared with red and black mud marks and no amount of red polish scrubbed on by sweaty servants using coconut husks made a difference. What pleased us most was to see the England returns with their pointed shoes slipping on the mud and falling or screaming as their ready-made clothes were splattered.

My mother was driven insane by the dirt in Mwanza and her lack of control over it. Fastidious to this day (she even folds her knickers), she would be waiting at the door as we all came in at the end of the day happy, tired and gloriously dirty. She would stand us outside in the yard or the veranda and with a tin pour water from a bucket all over us until it ran sort of clean.

There were family dramas here too. My sister Didi teamed up with my cousin Tahira – a young woman whose ravishing looks were considered a curse and every time they disappeared my mother quite rightly feared the worst. She knew that by the mid-fifties, the obedience and conformity which was deeply embedded in the lives of women of her generation, was being challenged by their daughters. Even the Hindi films were moving on from wearisome saintly heroines who wept and sang about the plight and joy of being downtrodden to actresses like the doe-eyed Nargis who wore trousers and in one film turned two men mad with desire by flirting shamelessly with them.

As yet, though, the really dangerous influences like Connie Francis had not arrived. But the signs were not good. By the mid-fifties people were aware and fearful that the safety of unchallenged truths and norms was under threat. The old folk would mutter about how young people now even looked you in the face when you were talking to them and asked for reasons – can you believe it? Then they would recall with affection: 'If I even looked at my father, he would beat me to a pulp. That is called respect. And the girls they were so obedient.'

As ever, the defence of the order was taken up by our young men and even in the easygoing families in Mwanza we had tensions developing between my boy cousins and their newly found mission to maintain the *izzat* of the house, (mainly by controlling the girls). The girls, of course, were far more cunning than the boys could ever be and they found a thousand ways of meeting and even holding the odd hand with the lusty lads of Mwanza (who were insanely protective of their own sisters) many of whom hung around the houses not unlike the hyenas at night.

In spite of living in a bigger town, Didi was not as streetwise as our cousins. She just watched and didn't tell, and that in the eyes of our many paranoid relatives was just as bad, because the integrity of a family depended on a properly functioning information and spy network. The old, whoever they were, were always watching and reporting on what was going on and the young could easily be corrupted by bribes or threats to tell on those they knew of. The loss of this function and the power they wielded is deeply felt by our many old people now as they sit meekly in a corner in their homes in Britain or Canada unable to influence at all the behaviour of their children or even their talkback grandchildren.

By 1955, at the age of sixteen, Tahira's goings on with Karim, the naive but handsome son of a neighbour, had become the talk of the entire community. People were afraid of her flashing eyes, small waist, twirling skirts, bold talk and sexual presence. Karim was already too bewitched to be rescued, so the best thing, the elders decided, was to marry them off, sacrifice Karim then at least the other girls and boys would be safe. His intoxication wore off, only to be followed by deep disenchantment and that awful grip of impotent jealousy and drink. Then in time, death mercifully rescued him. He was only twenty-four.

These relatives in Mwanza were genuinely loving, and although interested in money, were far more interested in having a roaringly good time. Whenever we returned to

Kampala after our holiday, although we were usually ill with the many diseases endemic in a town full of dreaded standing pools of stagnant water, we could hardly bear the terrible sadness of our own home.

For many years, this happy atmosphere was reproduced in this family's house in Ealing. Five bedrooms and three bathrooms housed four couples, their children, my *maami* and all other lost or needy family members from near and afar. Alnoor, a young man with penetrating eyes and a carrier bag of possessions, came out of nowhere and announced that he had some connection, so he got put in a corner near the sewing machine. Every morning the milkman would leave a crateful of milk bottles and three dozen eggs, shaking his head with disbelief and perhaps some anxieties about whether this was a den of illegal immigrants. The fry-up would use up all the eggs by ten o'clock and many of the family wobble around now in their middle age, having finally learned (but not really being convinced) about cholesterol and All Bran. Fragmented into little warring sections, their mother who kept them together dead and gone, my cousins lament the passing of those truly good old days: '*Yaar*, we had a life then. Five cars outside, no worries. My wife making eighty *rotlis* fresh, all of us at the table, side by side, the different fingers of one hand.' It was the wives who fought a rearguard action to split up the family into separate units. There is a limit to how many *rotlis* you can make in one lifetime.

At the other end of the spectrum was my Ramzan chacha's family who lived in the affluent hills of Kampala. They represented the greedier, more vicious bunch who had followed the early immigrants as the whispering spread across the subcontinent of the beauty and wealth of East Africa. Stories about ivory, and other forms of easy money that it was possible to make, made overambitious people take off in huge numbers from India and the newly formed Pakistan, and scatter wherever there was the whiff of a possibility. Chacha and his brothers, my father's cousins, who were amongst those who swept in, used to describe those days. 'We were not soft then. We killed what we wanted to eat and the *golas*, you could whip them with *dhokis* and they did not raise their heads.' Chacha Ramzan was one of the cruellest men I had ever met, with eyes made of flint which only showed any delight when he was being violent to his servants, his wife or his sons, most of whom, like Shamsu, ended up being despicable themselves. It was delicious to watch his partial humiliation, when at the age of sixty one of his mistresses took him to court to claim her share of his malignant fortune. But he was rich and people bowed down to him, allowing him to bathe in undeserved self-love.

He was however in awe of my father who was learned and indifferent to money, and of my mother who refused to be a victim. He died in 1995. In his last days he was unable to move, but that did not stop him being ever more suspicious of the long line of relatives whom he knew he had wronged and who may well have had expectations. When he died my mother cried with guilt, because she had found it hard to muster pity for chacha Ramzan.

When we used to visit his family, which we did too often, we would all tiptoe around the room where he was sitting or snoring, his huge wild dog and cane by his side. It was not possible to laugh in that house. It was too awash with rancour, which went down from person to person, finally even affecting the vicious dog. His children feared and abhorred him and found a million ways of thwarting his inhuman rules and regulations. When he was snoring at night, the house would come alive with whispers and swishing petticoats as they got dressed to go out, jumping through the windows and grabbing and muzzling the dog before it could bark too loudly. Chacha had trained his dog so that it treated everyone else in the house as the enemy.

This is when his family brought out all the finery which they kept hidden from the mean eyes of their father. But like all caged animals, once out, these young kids were volatile, unpredictable and often in fights which would leave the boys bruised and bleeding, wounds they had to hide from their father the next day, fearing his beatings more than anything they had experienced on their wild nights out. Once in a while they did get found out, when someone mentioned seeing them at a party. I shall never forget the time this happened when we were there. The vicious thrashing with a thin long stick, the screams, his wife trying not to cry because that would provoke him even more, the locking of the victims hardly able to breathe into the corner room, and worst of all, his swift return to normality and the huge appetite he built up through these exertions.

My mother was convinced his inhumanity came from the fact that he refused to eat vegetables: 'Just meat every day, it hots the blood and brain. Try and give him some yogurt and *moong* or something once a week. It may help this temper.' Like all dictators, he loved order in his life. His many suits and shirts, which had to be just so, laid out every morning by a sullen wife. A freshly pressed thick white napkin which he would spread over his vast stomach when he got into the car so that the steering wheel that dug into him would not crease his expensive suits. His hairy arms sporting a gold watch and thick identity bracelets, and the final act of ritualistic humiliation: as he drove off, he would ask one of his children to get him a fresh red rose from the garden to stick into his lapel. The atmosphere would tangibly lift as he drove away and the days he did not come home for lunch were wonderful. What a way to live. I felt no envy of the big house and the ostentation, the big cars and the gold he compelled his family to wear whenever they went out so that they could reflect his wealth without ever taking any pleasure in it.

There were moments when I did feel Papa was a blessing. At least he wasn't chacha Ramzan and besides, I am sure a lot of what I am today comes from the uncertainty that surrounded my life with Papa nominally in charge of it. This is what has helped to make me aware, always beyond my years, happy but never wholly so, too concerned, says my son (who looks a lot like my father), of what can go wrong the next minute. And finally a dash of sadness which adds depth and piquancy to life.

When he went through terrible pain and loss chacha was forced to acknowledge that money could not protect you from everything and that there was such a thing as pain which could afflict even someone as hard as him. As time passed, though, he started retreating even more into a world where his only loving relationship was with money and where all human contact was kept at bay. Perhaps it helped him feel immortal. His detachment and indifference released his other children into a freedom they relished, and it was a freedom that even his meanness could not taint.

6

As I grew up, I began to understand the profound changes that were taking place in our community and how many of these in the end did not serve us well. They told me how in the early days, the chaos and dangers that confronted people meant that they had to shed the tight social and religious mores of the subcontinent. Survival and the searing ambition to make good was all that mattered. Through the thirties and forties, sexual liberties were taken, Asian men took up with African women, and women like Ma made their own destinies. By the time we were in the fifties, these freedoms had gone. A stiffness had set in in our attitudes and we started seeing the African as some kind of irredeemable barbarian. The only sexual relations with blacks then would be rich Asian businessmen going with black prostitutes, or invisible mistresses whose caramel-coloured children would walk with them on the streets, a quiet reminder of what was really going on.

The children of the black/Asian liaisons would be called *chotaras*, a word that we used to denigrate people and describe anyone who wore bright colours like luminous pink and green. Terror of contamination and failure encouraged the transformation of Asian women into porcelain ornaments, symbols of purity and wealth, exactly like middle-class Victorian women.

The Africans would leave their own children behind in some village because they had to earn a living and come over to tend and love ours unconditionally. It would have been beneath us to appreciate this. So we pretended that we were the ones bestowing the favours. As these children turned into adolescents, the love and trust they felt for their ayahs and 'boys' – as we called the male African servants – would turn to a cold familiarity and even contempt. Shamsu once slapped his sixty-year-old ayah, who had looked after him and then his children, for kissing his young son in front of him. I wonder why we were surprised when the odd ayah decided to leave, carrying away the gold bangles people had hidden in their cupboards or when servants failed to return after their leave even when there was money left to collect from their wages: 'Don't give them all their money when they go home,' the masters and mistresses used to say: 'They'll only drink. And then they will go somewhere else. Keep some back.' The horror and self-pity they felt when a servant left without warning or even when one failed to turn up to work for a single day was extraordinary. Some would turn hysterical, others would rush about in their cars looking desperately for a substitute. All would plot their revenge. Zora Masi was the one who felt these moments most deeply and personally, partly because she was obsessive about cleanliness – her servants would wipe the tables and chairs while you were eating, gathering up crumbs and wiping droplets as they fell: 'Jenabai,' she would wail to my mother: 'What am I going to do? He hasn't shown up for two days. My blood pressure has gone up, I'm going to become mad. Why does God have to punish me in this way? You can never trust these blacks. Treat them like your children and they are still like this.' Some children.

But what astonishes me in retrospect is how, in spite of these attitudes and the resentment we were building up in those around us, we continued to feel at peace with ourselves. The fifties were a kind of oasis between monumental historical upheavals. We knew, as my mother now says, where we would be buried. We all had our places and there was no crossing of boundaries and hence no squabbles. 'That was the life, you know,' says Sadru, a family friend, these days, retired early after a heart attack caused by the shock of moving here and working on the buses. 'All the time we were so happy and having a *badshai* life. Servants to do everything, costing nothing, sitting outside, taking the air in the evening.'

Then as now, we seemed incapable of understanding the turmoil around our heads or the deep sense of peril growing in our hearts as we lived our stratified lives, only ever insecure about what the African was going to steal from us and how, whatever we had, it could never make us as grand as the *wazungu*.

There were white areas, white schools and shops on the main road which sold not only hats but ready-made dresses, initially for white memsahibs, but in time to women like Parin's sister – rich, spoilt England returns who made our lives miserable with envy. I had my first ready-made dress in 1966, a present from my brother after he had been to England for a holiday – mauve polyester it was, with a sailor collar and neat perm pleats. The joy of possessing that dress surpassed even the thrill of my first wet kiss, which happened when I was in fact wearing it. Enterprising vegetable sellers in the market would shout 'Nyloni beans mama, the bananas are Terylene.' We were all gullible – colonialism had inflicted a deep sense of inferiority in us, blinding us to the beauty of our own souls.

The blindness persists and continues to make puppets of us. The pull of England thus was ever present and although most of us were discerning enough not to want to be English – even the most naive of us had worked out that there was something sterile in the white bwanas and memsahibs we saw at a distance – to be a part of that world was a desire that corrupted all our hearts.

I remember feeling the anguish of childish craving as my best friend, Lily, who had more money than we did, brought imported apples in her lunch-box and Kraft cheese sandwiches. I took a chappati rolled around whatever was left from the previous day, and I hated it, especially after Mrs Marks, a pretentious Goan teacher whose legs were always smeared with white shoe colour, remarked in her sharp voice through pursed lips on how I should brush my teeth after lunch because of the terrible smell: 'or better still, tell your mother to give you sandwiches, like Lily'.

The coronation in 1953 was the moment when all this came together in one massive wave. As we stood under the searing sun, in our pristine school uniforms which slowly began to drip and cling, making us itch in unscratchable places, waving the Union Jack and watching the band march past, we knew something momentous was happening but that it somehow excluded us. Our parents made cursory attempts to join in, because it was considered expedient, by hanging up calendars with pictures of the queen in a tiara. These were left there for years to fade away slowly. I loved that picture. And also the little tins we got from school, all royal purple and festooned with flowers and regalia. Each tin contained a pencil, eraser, sharpener, a few Cadbury's chocolates, and the words of 'God Save the Queen'.

Most of the Africans seemed indifferent to these tantalising breezes that blew into our lives from Britain. Only the elite who were being moulded into proper public schoolboys by the top missionary schools felt an affinity for the home country. Those Asians who came from communities which kept a tight hold on their connections with India and Pakistan, often by going back there for three months every year, also seemed immune to the heartbreaking longings that infiltrated the lives of those of us who were less sure of what or who we were. The pressure to change was also increasing.

The old Aga Khan decided that it was important for our community to move with the times. An anglophile himself, he asked the women in the community to discard their saris, long gowns and scarves and start wearing Western-style dresses. Overnight, the women in mosque had to cope with showing their arms and legs in public as they squirmed in dresses which many had not worn since they were young girls. Sitting on the mats in mosque was a particularly terrifying ordeal. So developed the fashion for wide, ankle-length dresses, and for the first time the dilemma of whether, how and why one should get rid of the hair on the legs. Bold and brazen women who had been stifled by convention in the past took the opportunity to lower their necklines and even display their upper arms.

Funnily enough it was the older women who proudly revealed their cleavages and I saw, for the first time, how wanton and out of control big breasts could make you look. Later, when I developed a bosom which was large enough to be always noticeable because I was tiny in other ways, I had psychotic fantasies about chopping them off every time I saw them wobbling at me in the mirror. But this disgust was mild compared to the fury my father felt when he saw what the women were doing to themselves. It was a fury that emanated from different sources. Partly it was his Victorian values that made him genuinely horrified and disturbed by how quickly the forces of dissolution could take hold. Partly it was because his own peculiar view of pure and chaste womanhood was being defied and defiled. And partly it was an affront to his aesthetic sense. When Jumu uncle and his plump wife who was nicknamed Mama Football came to visit in the evenings, Papa would explode at her when she bent down to pour the tea in her low-necked dress, her ample bosom almost entirely on display and several gold chains tangled up and lost in the floppy flesh: 'Jumu, take shame, what is this? Have you no control over your wife?' he roared. 'You have to have the body, the shape to wear frocks. Tell her to go back to her saris, to look decent. Tell her, man.' There they were, the double standards of my father. A deep conservatism plus a brave unconventionality, a whole series, in fact, of muddled messages. His manic obsessions with the West, but a dread of contamination by the forces of the West and of course the lingering romanticism of women draped in flowing saris. It was this romanticism that made him lust after my mother when he saw her sweeping the yard, a shy young girl of sixteen, and it was the realisation that he needed something else that made him impatient with her from day one.

Poor Jumu uncle. He was a simple and kind man with a heart of gold, a motor mechanic who could barely read and write, whose nails were always black and who always respected my father far too much because this is what being learned was all about: 'He is right, you know, this Kassam. This is education, you see?' But however much peculiar admiration people like this might have felt, it was not enough to influence their deep religious faith or their absolute devotion to the words of the imam. And a good thing too. What was the point of having an original approach to life if it left you stranded and dislocated? Jumu uncle's children followed in his tradition, failed miserably at school, excelled at mending cars and are now living like kings in America. They still gather and pray every day, with the fifteen other Ismailis in a small town in Pennsylvania, in a room above the garage which they have made into a pretty little mosque – a peaceful place full of fresh flowers and incense.

Asians are good at that sort of thing. Taking religion, cultural quirks, anything that connects you for ever to the last place you thought was your real home. In Kampala we managed in a few years to turn the town into a neverending statement of our presence. The Hindu festivals were the most assertive. Diwali, and for days the sounds of women singing and dancing in their shimmering saris and the smells of cooking would pervade the streets. (These days you can see this happening in Wembley on a less grand scale, although it has to be said that no amount of joyful greetings or offerings of sweetmeats seem to be able to elicit even a smile from the large number of traffic wardens to be found in the area.)

At night the whole town would be ablaze with fireworks of every description. Groups would have battles hurling bangers at each other across the street. Boys and girls grabbed precious moments of body contact — a youthful hand grabbing an exposed waist, or stroking hair allowed to stay untied only for very special occasions — afraid that a cousin or brother would see them, especially at those moments when the street blazed open with the light of a particularly spectacular firework. It was a miracle that so few people got injured. Or caught. There was a wonderful, if incomprehensible, marrying at this time of worldly and otherworldly interests, and I think the rich genuinely began to believe not only that God had ordained it that they should get even more prosperous but that they were actually sitting closer to the lap of the gods by having become richer than they were the year before. None of this guilt-inducing or placating stuff about the poor entering the kingdom of heaven first.

Then came Holi which meant people running riot in town hurling coloured water which never washed off. Chaturbhai, the man who sold made-in-England shirts, took a holiday on that day. My favourite event was Rakhi day, when if you were a Hindu you declared your undying love for your brother by giving him a bracelet made of felt and glitter. He, in turn, would give you money and swear to be a good brother in the following year. It was an affirmation that I loved, though my own brother, not being Hindu and being supercool, would not have welcomed it at all.

Canny girls used *rakhis* to thwart boys who were pestering them for romantic favours. Smiling sweetly they would hand over the *rakhis* and declare that henceforth they were their lifetime brothers. Something as sacrosanct as that could never again be broken and the stuttering disappointed lad would have to look elsewhere. Manu (MTEH, we called him, Manu The Ever Hopeful), one of the most ardent romantics in town, and also one of the most undesirable if one discounted his flash green car, was given more *rakhis* than anybody else, and he would parade his broken heart by wearing all of them on his spindly arm which he stuck out of his window as he drove his car around slowly whilst singing morbid Mohamed Rafi songs until he spied the next girl to chase and offer himself to.

Even on an ordinary Sunday, on the streets you felt like you were in Bombay (one of the excuses used by the odious President Amin when he announced our expulsion), with Hindi music blaring out, people dressed in their best clothes parading up and down the two main streets, making eyes at each other and allowing themselves to look for illicit pleasures if only in their heads.

Yes, life was indeed *badshai* for a while and it made us forget ourselves and the pain it was causing others.

Our lives at home too had acquired some kind of equilibrium and stability. My mother had gained her place in the various communities and was always surrounded by friends. She was the last to leave mosque, much to the annoyance of whoever she had cornered into giving her a lift that night. She always wore saris, never any makeup – another order from my father, who recoiled from a made-up woman as if she was diseased – and just a tiny bit of perfume that she had been given years ago by some grateful customer. With the little money she had, she managed to dress us all so we never felt ashamed at least on the outside and at times even proud when the curious combinations of buttons and bows created a spectacularly original design which made the rich women in our community, those with expensive pearls and doting, successful husbands, ask her to make some for their children.

Yes, things were really looking up around the time I was eight; I remember feeling awash with contentment. My Amir had returned, disgruntled because he'd had to give up his A-level courses, but back. He loved me almost insanely and spoilt me with presents bought with his own money. Even imported lychees one day. What further proof did I need of love? He started work when he came back and my mother found a little respite with regular wages coming in. He dressed like a dandy, whizzed through life on a high, and even saved up to buy a record player. For Papa the music and the joy were too much to bear. As Babu lay on the floor listening to Miles Davis, my father would start mumbling about the noise and the money he had wasted on his son. If this had no effect he would increase his nagging and then start shouting until he had driven Babu out of the house. We were living on borrowed happiness. I felt for my brother and knew we would lose him again, having only so recently had him back.

As Amir prospered, my father seemed to wither a little bit more with hostility and a growing sense that he was a loser.

But it did not stop him making erratic decisions. There was still little money left over so my sister had taken Babu's place in England. My father was convinced that girls needed to be better educated than boys, who would make it anyway. Babu quite rightly felt rebuffed and deprived. My sister was elated and went off with unbearable pleasure. For many years I imagined the whole of England to be like Poole, Dorset, because of all the windswept pictures my sister sent back. She came to visit once and she had changed into a woman. I could hardly recognise her as the skinny girl with long plaits and an angelic face who had left us not that long ago. After a few months, she disappeared from my life. Nobody mentioned her name. Her lovely photographs which had hung proudly on the back of the wooden doors and on the walls also inexplicably seemed to vanish. By the time I met her again in 1972, she was a changed person, the bloom on her gone for ever and people who met her unable to understand where that beauty and innocence had fled. There was also a bright and beautiful little daughter, my niece, whom nobody had talked about before.

A couple of years after Didi left, a new kind of despair began to settle among the four corners of our small flat. There were muffled rows in the bedroom which seemed intensely acrid. My father locked himself away in the bedroom, in his pyjamas. Endless cigarettes and his thoughts were his only friends. Whenever he interjected into our lives, he would disrupt the harmony and the joy. His looks became more vacant and suspicious and he seemed to be seeing dangers that did not exist. His eyes would scrutinise everything I was wearing to see that it was respectable and although I learned to avoid those piercing eyes, I felt his presence, his intense gaze on me long after I had left him.

But as time went on, I grew stronger and this morbid atmosphere in our house seemed to affect me less and less. I was ten, popular at school, picking up friends who had more than I had but who always seemed willing to share, and like my mother who had to find an alternative world, I too learned to survive.

The school I went to was another reason for my increasing sense of stability and joy. A new headmaster and his wife, the Bagchis, had arrived from Calcutta to run it. They were both larger than life, highly intellectual, passionate about the theatre and the arts, bursting with ideas and exuberance, but deeply mistrustful of each other because they could not assess how far, if unleashed, their sensuality would stray. She was voluptuous, shameless about the space she occupied in the world, daring people to challenge this as she swung about in her saris, her rasping voice and her sharp eyes ready to pounce on anyone acting out of place whilst always inviting them to do so. An enchantress, what's more, married to a spellbindingly hand-some man with a deep dark voice which he used not to threaten but cajole and persuade all those around him.

We fell in love with both of them and their three children, who seemed to us to belong to quite another world from that inhabited by the other Asians for whom life consisted of work, wealth, religion, families, Hindi films and endless visits to and from relatives and friends. We yearned to be noticed and approved of by them. We wanted their slightly odd, supercili-ous children (one who was forever walking around with feet turned outwards because she wanted to be a ballerina and others who stuck up their painted leaves and sticks on the clean white walls of their living room, *imagine that*, without being castigated by houseproud parents) to show some passing interest in us. Three of us – Lily, my friend with the Kraft cheese sandwiches, Vera, a Parsee girl, who spoke English better than any of us because her parents were able to, unlike most of ours, and I – did manage to find favour. This enabled us to look down on and laugh at the other children in our class, even those who could do arithmetic and whose help we were constantly seeking.

The Bagchis wrote plays and acted in major productions at the National Theatre, which until then had been a white outpost forbidden to the rest of us. They brought drama into our lives. An unforgettable occasion was the staging of *A Midsummer Night's Dream* by the ex-pats drama group. Ganesh and Kuku Bagchi enticed their way in and took over the production. As Titania and Oberon they played out the jealousies of their own lives with seething feeling, beguiling and dangerous at the same time. Six of us were chosen to play the fairies, all in green with tight tops over pubescent breasts and tiny midriffs on display. Our parents did not, could not, object, so daunted were they by what they presumed to be an essential part of an excellent European education.

We had a glorious time – late nights and close proximity for the first time to white people who were not dressed in khaki and did not have dead eyes like the administrators one saw driving past or the school health inspectors who came looking for lice and then grumbled because you had oily hair which smelt of stale coconut. They too adored the Bagchis, in ways which bordered on lechery, partly because these Indians seemed not to be in awe of them at all. I was quite overwhelmed by their audacity. The only time I had seen people socialising with whites was when some mild form of corruption or enticement was being offered to a bank manager, especially at Christmas time. Even then, the manner was slavish and insincerity was thick in the air.

The Bagchis recruited teachers into the school who also had glamour and brave new ideas. In fact the school was linked to the teacher training college and so all kinds of innovative schemes – not all brilliant – arrived in our lives long before they reached other schools in the country. Roxy was another favourite. A sophisticated Parsi woman who wore pencil-thin skirts over tempting buttocks (this is what we heard male teachers saying about them), she played the piano and wrote banal songs which she injected into our annual school plays. One year she produced *Cinderella*. Lily and I were Drusilla and Priscilla, the ugly sisters. At the end we all had to sing:

> Cinderella's to be wed
> By the prince she'll be led
> To the aisle, to the aisle on Friday morn.

And we thought it was all 'out of this world' and 'simply super'. You see, by now we were also beginning to read *Bunty*, that girls' comic which told you about midnight feasts at English boarding-schools. I proved that I could act better than the girl who played Cinderella could look, so in the next production I got to be Scheherazade.

> Scheherazade, we sing in joy for Scheherazade,
> Scheherazade, she's brought such happiness to everyone,
> Our days are now filled with joy and fun,
> Because of Scheherazade

Shamsu's wife donated her wedding sari – which she felt was an inauspicious garment and about which she was quite rightly completely unsentimental – for us to make into a beautiful costume with billowing trousers and a veil. Come to think of it, perhaps this is why Roxy let me play the heroine. Behind a semi-transparent veil, it was easy to conceal the fact that I was no great beauty. This was also the beginning of people telling me that I should be very proud because I had personality and intelligence (in other words I was not pretty but there was hope).

My father was almost pleased for a short while then, as he saw me blossoming into a young girl who could recite entire chunks from the great English writers and who consistently won British Council elocution contests because unlike the other Asian children I could say 'p' and 't' with a proper puff. Six tedious hours, while seventy of us recited 'Do you Remember an Inn, Miranda . . . ?' or even worse, good manners rhymes like

> It is as well to remember,
> No elbows on the table please,
> Nor is a cup, one understands,
> So heavy that it needs both hands.

A line of self-important Englishmen and women would sit through this, showing no emotion and inevitably mispronouncing the Asian and African names as they called out the next victim. At the end, a brief statement would announce the three winners in the three categories and we would get a book and a handshake which thrilled us immeasurably and gave us pride to take back to our anxious parents who were not allowed to attend the events.

By this time, mainly because my brother had been making more money as a smooth-talking insurance salesman, we could afford to move to a bigger apartment near the school. The block was called Century House. It was a lovely place with red polished floors and the apartment had two bedrooms. Papa felt increasingly insignificant and angry that his son was taking over the role of supporting the family he had so often sought to run away from. The balance of power changing in this way was painful to watch, especially as his harder edge was beginning to show in my brother at the same time. Papa felt impotent with his son. His older daughter was out of range, somewhere else. I was the only one he could have any control over and so I became a focus for him in a way which began to suffocate me.

I remember his insane rage when I made the mistake of

coming home after a performance of a school play with my stage makeup still on: 'You'll end up in disgrace. Don't listen to me, you never do, you will regret it one day and remember me. You have no future, you stupid girl.' I didn't regret it, I never have. And so far, I don't think I have disgraced myself in any way that would make him turn in his grave. On days like this, because he was like a wild but incapacitated animal who would not listen, I could be reduced to hot tears by this man. It wasn't the fact that I had disappointed him or that he hurt me with his utterly unfair assaults; it was simply that he did not respect what I was. But I guess I must have been deeply afraid of what he had prophesied because not only did I never dare not to come top in school and university, but I never ever experimented with rudimentary sexual experiences the way my more sophisticated friends managed to without being found out. And they were allowed to wear lipstick. Believe me that wasn't easy for a girl who had no pouting pretty face to offer nor a house with vast lawns and servants to serve Coke while you listened to pop music, nor any connections, which is how everything worked in Uganda.

Papa got worse when he found out that my newest and most special friend, Naseem, was the daughter of an Asian woman, Mumtaz, who owned and ran a bar. Every evening Mumtaz would walk past the building where we lived, wearing her see-through sari and sleeveless blouse, on her way to the bar. I am sure she swung her hips unnecessarily emphatically as she passed our house, though she never looked up. Every evening my father would be waiting for her on the balcony and he would let off a stream of abuse just soft enough so she could not hear. Papa was becoming cowardly as he lost his early assurance that he was always a somebody even when his family was penniless.

Then would come a lecture about how I was not allowed to speak to Naseem any more. But he could not stop me, not even with the frenzy he put on specially after he had seen us together. Naseem and I were a pair for a couple of years and I think I stuck with her just to defy my father. In fact I hated her because she was so very pretty with her smooth skin and dimples (she was Cinderella when I was an ugly sister) and she hated me because I was cleverer and funnier than anybody else she had ever known. But Naseem and I shared a deeper bond than either of us realised. We both came from families which lacked status and respectability. We both had mothers who could challenge convention, albeit in a sweet way, until the community got tired of gossiping about them and simply embraced them in the end, providing some kind of a space. On the periphery.

Although we had moved away from her, my mother and I still went to see Ma every Saturday after we had been to the market. She would wait until we got there and then bark out orders for tea and snacks to be made. Zubine and Almira seemed more and more oppressed and they would cry when they saw my mother because at least when she was nearby she would stand up for them and comfort them when things got unbearable. Zubine once had a black eye when we went for tea. My mother finally took on Ma and told her that however much she indulged Allah, he could see what she was doing to these women and he would not forgive her. There was a roaring silence as Ma puffed on her cigarette and looked out of the open door overlooking the street. Then she turned and said quietly to my mother: 'If you feel so sorry for this barren one, why don't you marry her to your son?' My mother was stunned by the poison in her words and voice. We got up to leave. Zubine came in, her eyes streaming with tears, begging my mother not to go. Ma looked at us with her flinty grey eyes and told my mother not to waste the tea and to sit down. To add insult to injury, she gave me money and chocolates as we left. Zubine called out to say that she would be waiting the following Saturday and to tell Papa that she and Almira missed him. Yes, in their harsh and cruel lives they even missed Papa, who found it hard to cope with deliberate cruelty and had once locked them in our flat, refusing to let them out until Ma promised to treat them better.

He was always capable of these generous and kind gestures. Ones that didn't cost him anything. Like the time he gave away my brother's brand new shoes and jacket to a *maskini* who came to the door. Japan, for the first time since he started working for us, was accused by Amir of stealing his things and within an hour he left our house never to be seen again. His last words to my brother were about how he had become 'bad-hearted' since going to England.

It was months later that my father confessed what he had done, defiantly arguing that the beggar needed the things more than any of us did. My father, the rudimentary socialist.

But he still dared to show off and show us off. His bravado got worse as he became more and more incapable of work and depended in a pathetic way on his son, pleading for cigarettes. I felt awful for him when he begged and then stormed off saying he would never ask for anything again and came back the very next day. Sometimes he would get me to ask Amir for money. Amir would pour scorn sometimes, play the dutiful son at other times, always a game. Like the games he played with the servants on Sundays, later when he was richer and he had a car in which he would only ever offer to give any of us a lift when he needed to feel virtuous.

At three o'clock on a Sunday, just as John or Mary were leaving all shiny faced, Amir would call them back: 'Hey John, there is a mark on the car, wash it off. John, make some tea before you go, get me a beer.' They could say nothing. For ninety shillings a month, they were yours. Dead souls. The game I found hardest to play was the one that required me to wait for days before getting the twelve shillings I needed for my school fees, which we both knew he had in his pocket. But even during these trying times, I knew that inside him there was still some love for me. I have always known that.

My mother too was struggling against this new person her adored son was turning into. She became a prisoner of her love

72

for him and the money he could afford to give her each month, which was never enough. She could no longer supplement the income though. It would be too shameful for a family which was now trying to move up the social ladder. In part this helped my mother to pretend to herself and others that here at last was a man taking responsibility for her, the way all her friends took for granted but which she had only been able to watch enviously from a distance. In part it made her feel wretchedly dependent for the first time in her life. I had never before seen my mother putting on an act that was not a practical necessity to keep the debtors at bay or persuade long-suffering rationwallahs to let us have a little more on credit. These days, looking as if we had gone up in the world and trying to live within the tight circle of respectability, there was no more credit to be asked for or given. Behind closed doors, she would teach me how to make sanitary pads from old sheets and how to wash them out in private.

Muljibhai, our doctor who had always treated our family without demanding the instant payment all the other, more competent doctors did, started to worry about the stress my mother was under. She cried unprovoked, lost weight, looked vulnerable and frightened and began to age fast: 'The burdens on my head, they just increase. God, I must have done something terrible in my past life.' She started a collection of pills and potions. In the tiny council flat in Ealing where she now lives, she has antique medicines which go back to the 1940s. She will not throw them away, 'just in case'. You only have to mention an ailment and out come the boxes with the ointments, syrups which have darkened ominously with time, but which she still insists are fine, the little pink pills that 'Muljibhai once gave me for headaches/giddy spells/tiredness/the menopause/depression', or that ubiquitous problem that is the favourite of all Asian women, blood pressure and insomnia. I have heard my mother snoring so loud that it has kept me up – and it takes a lot to keep me awake – and yet the next day she will say and believe that she hardly slept at all, 'even with all the

73

strongest tablets, you know the doctor is so surprised when I am telling him that problem of my sleep'. But I laugh now because those days are mercifully far away. The truly despondent days when my mother's spirit finally seemed to be captured.

7

Century House opened our lives up to other kinds of people who made up the Asian community and also to their many loud, poisonous and screaming battles. This had gone on in our previous home of course, but because there was very little real animosity between the families, the fights were simply reassuring rituals that all the protagonists had become used to and probably could not do without; they were a way of testing the bonds that existed between them. So, my mother would complain about the noise of the *kasookoo* to Ma and Ma would tell her that even she could not control the behaviour of a bird. My mother would feel guilty and go and feed extra-hot red chillis to the parrot, who loved them passionately and would reward us with even more noisy songs and endlessly repeated phrases like: 'Jena, Jena bai, mirchi de.' – 'Give me a chilli.'

Shantaben Desai, before she had absconded to India, would smile softly and ask the Muslims not to cook their meat in a pressure cooker because she threw up for hours afterwards and could not eat. Ma, who had little respect for people who tried to survive on a bloodless diet, would coldly say that she too had felt nauseous when the dull, pervasive smell of dhal permeated the building. Then she would mutter not all that under her breath, that these *banyanis* were the same, and that not eating meat made them unable to withstand anything robust because their blood was too thin. Shantaben, a quiet little woman, would leave, still smiling sweetly, and would reappear with a plateful of food saying something genuinely nice like: 'Why should we fight, we are just on a short journey in this world.'

One day when Shantaben had a bad headache, Ma sent her a bowl of chicken soup, with a message carried by innocent little Khatun that she should force herself to have some as if she was 'drinking medicine'. Poor Shantaben had to virtually fumigate the house – to render it properly pure and chaste – after she had thrown away the soup, plate and all.

For days afterwards, she looked hurt and kept well away from the Muslim flats until my mother went to see her pretending that she wanted to learn how to make her magically effective recipes for tooth powder and laxatives.

But even at their worst, these quarrels were never destructive. In contrast, what happened in the fifty flats in Century House, was truly vicious and long lasting. Perhaps this was because there was no possibility of real intimacy. People left the back door open and shouted their business and what was not their business across to each other. Discreet gossip and whispering secret observations would have been too time-consuming and tiring, what with all those stairs separating the families. So, in the daytime, you heard the women bellowing across to each other, complaining about their husbands and the increasingly disrespectful behaviour of their children. Intermittently, and especially during the holidays, you would hear the bloodcurdling screams of one of these children as they got a thrashing for something or other. Floor-sweepers made of long grass were a favourite weapon. The best escape was to run up to the roof where you could hide among the water tanks and where neither the slothful nor the exhausted mothers would bother to follow. Not infrequently, the moans about husbands would abruptly stop and you would know that either the man himself or more likely his adoring mother had appeared on the scene. Up among the water tanks we would pretend to be ballerinas.

Rosie was different. For one thing she was white and living in flats that were only really meant to be for Asians. What was even more scandalous was that she was married to an Asian – a Goan named Roger, a skinny, amiable man whose skin was almost jet black. This was the first such mixed marriage we had ever come across and before people actually began to know the family, much of the shouting across the flats would be (mostly invented) stories about this strange couple. Nusratbai was the one who was most creative: 'He gave her something to drink, you know, that sort of thing, that Zanzibari mixture. Allah Allah, *tobah tobah*. It makes you follow anything, even a dog. Such a beautiful girl, what is she doing with this black Goan?' When her daughter told her about *A Midsummer Night's Dream*, Nusratbai was even more convinced about the story she had made up while she was cooking for her very demanding family. When Rosie openly cuddled her husband as they walked up the stairs, Nusratbai recited a prayer and averted her eyes.

People in Uganda at this time did not marry across the races, communities, religions or even sub-groups. In our community those who spoke Kutchi did not marry other Ismailis who spoke Gujarati. Kutchi speakers were regarded as devious, envious and mean. Gujarati speakers were simple-minded, carriers of weak genes and worst of all, indolent. My mother was a Gujarati and my father Kutchi. To many people this was all one needed to know in order to understand why things just never seemed to work between them. I wonder how many times parents used the example of my family to dissuade their young from marrying across this absurd divide.

It is all too easy to think in these ways. I know that when I wanted to understand the depth of antagonism between me and my sister-in-law, even I came to believe that there must be some truth in these caricatures. She was a proper Kutchi, grasping and selfish, and she did despise us. We were then her simple-minded victims. In this way, we could justify the very real animosity we felt for her. The outsider, the one who took our Amir away. And the man came across as a saint, a martyr:

the tortured soul, head in his whisky glass, surrounded by possessive, hysterical women. I wonder if we would have been kinder to a more gentle woman, or whether we would have had to invent a beast, whoever had come into our family.

Other taboos were even more insurmountable. Marrying right out, for example. The first time I became aware of this was when Dinker Patel killed himself by drinking concentrated sulphuric acid from the school lab. Dinker was our science teacher in primary school. A debonair young man who loved to make himself look and feel good, he wore beautiful clothes, had a hairstyle like the Everly Brothers, wore pointed shoes with metal tips, smelt of expensive imported lotions, walked with a swing. He was a Hindu. His tragedy was that he fell in love with a beautiful Sikh woman training to be a teacher who had come to the school for her teaching practice. Her brothers found out and the next day she was gone, taken off to the Punjab somewhere. Dinker was found dead by the caretaker, and for days afterwards we heard gory details of how much disintegration his body had suffered. Poor Dinker, they all said, he should have known better than to go for a Sikh. And what is all this love business? See how much trouble it brings. *Yaar*, the old ways are the gold ways.

Romantic love is what they were talking about. Something that was beginning to seep into our lives quietly and all the more dangerously for that reason. In the late forties, Hindi films had abandoned worthy religious and mythological stories for endlessly tortuous tales of forbidden/thwarted/betrayed/mis-understood/consuming love. Stars fell madly and sincerely in love (*pyar*). They ran around trees, sniffed at flowers and watched sunsets, the rising moon, the fountains. They sang incessantly. They coyly touched the tips of their fingers. They did not kiss, but you were usually shown two candle flames licking each other or a bird pecking at a dark red rose, and you knew. *Pyar* then conquered caste and class barriers, parental objections, and obstacles put in the lovers' way by big-bellied villains with long moustaches usually with cigarettes nearly falling out of the side of their snarling mouths. The protagonists married. She became a virtuous daughter-in-law and put up with the tyrant in-laws until they saw their evil ways or she died. All these events had appropriate songs which we learned off by heart and still sing whenever times are hard or unbelievably good.

In their own way these films were already subverting existing social mores and especially the pillar of strictly arranged marriages. But in the end these were fantasies and were not meant to infiltrate real lives where conformity to 'tradition' was the only continuity and stability we had. People like Dinker had clearly failed to understand this.

But although we were not meant to run around trees declaring our love, we were meant to learn the deeper lessons of life. That real women showed their mettle by suffering in silence and standing by their men. That overtly sexual women were all nightclub dancers who drank Black Label whisky and got themselves killed in the end-of-film fires which consumed evil. That respecting and obeying your parents and then your in-laws was next to godliness.

This is why I tried so hard (or maybe pretended) to be the perfect daughter-in-law and wife too. It was not easy especially when the other side of me was capable of hurling books and (empty) teacups at my husband. When one brother-in-law ended up staying with us for months – the one who drank himself into a state of misery every evening (giving his empty whisky boxes to my baby son to play with) and demanded fresh chappatis at ten in the evening – my already bitten fingers began to bleed. And then he boasted he was going to find a case of gold under a tree hidden by some general in Uganda, information he had picked up in a bar in Canada where lost men tried to find reasons to go back 'home'. We were expected to chip in to buy his tickets because he was family. At those times I felt like a saint in drag.

I hated it but to admit hate would have been such a defeat for someone trying to be Meena Kumari, a popular Indian actress who excelled at playing the tearful martyr. But for a few years, intermittently, I lived up to those ideals of the old Hindi films. These days the films are dreadful: men and women in revealing clothes, going to bed together, the women behaving like Madonna. Now I know this is deeply hypocritical for someone who still wears the odd miniskirt and long sexy slash up a black skirt, but I cannot bear these films. They blaspheme against my memories, the purity that I fantasise we all might have had if we hadn't been mucked up by history.

My mother made friends with Rosie using wide smiles, handshakes, titbits that she persuaded her to taste and morsels of English she had managed to pick up. It was only after she came to England that my mother learned to communicate in English, mainly through reading *Woman* magazine at a painstakingly slow rate, and watching children's television. But my mother has a natural empathy with the lost of this world, and bit by bit she discovered the true story about these two misfits, who as a result attached themselves to her.

Rosie was the daughter of a firebrand South African preacher who was staying at the hotel where Roger was the catering manager. He had been selected because he specialised in Anglo-Indian curries which used bananas and marmalade to placate the palates of white folk unused to extreme tastes but eager to have something adventurously different. Reverend Samson roared at everyone, but Roger, who was meek and obliging and was, after all, some kind of Christian, like all Goans.

In fact the Goans in East Africa were the ideal intermediaries for the British in lots of other ways too. They were genuinely humble, pious *and* they spoke grammatically correct English, but with an accent that we found easy to mock because it was full of hard consonants and a lilt that distinguished them from the real English. But our mocking had little effect. They thought they were the chosen ones because they were. They were selected for all the low-grade administrative jobs set up by the British and they also tended to be headmasters and headmistresses of big Asian schools where they treated the pupils like so many heathens and where they were mercilessly laughed at behind their backs because of their clothes, the dark chocolate colour of their skins, and the excruciating thinness of their legs. Like that awful Mrs Marks, my teacher, who abused my lunch-box at every opportunity and who also once brought cold sausage rolls and passed them round with a look that was so fierce that we all felt bound to eat them and then suffer that thick stickiness on the top palate that lard in pastry leaves behind.

I never told my mother that I had eaten them, knowing her views on people who eat 'pigs'. They not only smell different, she claims, but they are hard-hearted men and women who put their babies into nurseries and their old people into nursing homes. These days when she feels wronged by me, it is always the bacon in the fridge which is tucked right at the back that she blames. I still find it necessary to deny that I eat it. All her life the rational side to my mother has tried to find practical reasons for certain religious beliefs. In part this is so she can appear less superstitious than all her friends, whom she likes to describe as nice but a little too much into blind faith, a little ignorant. Unlike her. The dictum 'You are what you eat' was taken literally in this society.

Roger charmed Rosie with his brand of inoffensive and peaceful masculinity. They fell in love, and dutifully told the Reverend. He erupted, tried to thrash the petrified Roger, who being a fit young man escaped, followed by a jubilant Rosie who had found her kind of man at last. As different as could humanly be possible from her red-faced, gross and terrifying father, whom she despised deeply, especially because he claimed to have the ear of God. Just like Ma and Ramzan chacha. Roger's family also disowned him for not knowing his proper place. His mother came over once and only once and the entire neighbourhood went quiet as she shouted at him, refusing even to cross the threshold: 'Your father would feel such shame, the British they trusted us always. He would not look at a British woman in the face. That is respect. What was wrong with that nice Victoria, Mr Desouza's daughter? Goes to church, makes jams for the Ladies' Club, decent, good modest family. Good dressmaker too. Just brought shame on all of us.'

The hotel sacked Roger and forwarded a letter in which Samson threatened to return with a posse from South Africa to rescue his 'angel' from the jaws of the 'gorilla'. Roger showed me the letter, and we laughed over the idea of horses trying to climb up the narrow greasy stairs of Century House. Rosie didn't think it was at all funny. She was sure they would come one day and lynch her husband and the two sons she had produced in the interim, especially Tarquin who was just a pint-sized little Roger. She had bars put across their windows in the front of the flat. In fact they lived six floors up and the only living creatures who could peer in were the vultures and marabou stork that occasionally you would see flapping around because down the road was the main rubbish dump of the town.

When I went back home in 1994, the vultures and storks were still there, though much much bigger, less taciturn, and these days waddling about in a menacing way and only flying a few yards when absolutely essential. One street trader told me: 'The only things that have grown fat in Uganda are the vultures, and I don't only mean the birds.'

Mr Kantibhai Patel, the landlord, was not happy about the bars across the windows: 'It spoils the show, do you know how much we paid for this building?' He was always eager to tell us how much. 'Looks like a jail, *yaar*, like a damn bloody jail.' But he lacked the courage to confront a white woman.

Kantibhai would be heartbroken to see Century House today, with paint peeling off, bullet holes and shattered glass and, worst of all, clothes hanging outside on the balconies. This was something that tried him sorely when we lived there. Udyam House next door which was for posh people never had any clothes up and had terrazzo floors all shiny where rich ladies with patent black stiletto heels would clip their way to and from boutiques. The clothes they bought there obviously belonged to a strange brave new world, because they were never washed and hung out to dry. Kantibhai wanted our clothes to be at the back in the dark where they would not be seen. But we all knew better. The morning was an excellent time to hang out your clothes in the front because the sun would be on that side.

Rosie would provoke him deliberately by hanging out her frilly nylon panties and bras and he would complain bitterly and loudly up from the street, but in Gujarati so she could not understand. During these bouts he dwelt rather a lot on the shamelessness of white women, in particular blonde white women, who were all like Marilyn Monroe whose half-naked inviting pictures were seen in all sorts of disreputable places.

Kanti was braver with the many *maskinis* and *karanga* (peanut) sellers who had set up business underneath the building. He would kick their mats, their little baskets, swear at them and generally treat them like vermin until they shuffled away for a few hours and then as soon as he had gone, reappeared and went back to where they had left off, unperturbed by the scene. Their day came when a stork shat on his head, his crisply ironed safari suit and his overclean car just as he was getting out from his car to scream at them.

The trouble with this Mr Patel was that he wanted to be liked too much. Except by *maskinis* and small-timers. He must have also known that most people thought he was a simpleton with far too much inherited money for his own good. Even children had worked out that the way to deal with Kantibhai was to look down on him. Rosie knew how to keep him in his place by speaking to him just haughtily enough. At least half his tenants at any one time failed to pay their rent, and instead of theatening them he would beg and almost cry when he reminded them of the goodwill he had paid on the property. They would still not pay him and then mutter, as he walked away throwing some inept threat over his stooped shoulders, 'No guts this boy. Not like his father, that Jayantbhai. Now he was a giant. Such a pity he passed away. Business now going to the dogs in that boy's hands.' Jayantbhai would have had them all out on the streets too.

8

My father was, around this time, beginning to dream again of impossible things. Kantibhai was in the mood to listen to these one day when they were having a drink, well, several drinks, at City Bar. Together they hatched a plan. Papa came home, more animated than we had seen him in many months. He even had a proper conversation with my mother, repeating word for word what had passed between him and Kanti. 'Wong is tired of running his restaurant, you are a man of the world, sophisticated, you know the European people, you have worked with them at General Motors and African Mercantile. We are going to buy him out, you be the manager.' Either drink or a natural diffidence – he didn't speak English very well and was therefore convinced of his own abject inferiority – must have influenced him to make this extraordinary decision.

Papa had only ever failed spectacularly and he was almost indifferent to food. One fried egg on toast every night and everything else gobbled absent-mindedly at lunchtime was all that I remember about Papa and food. Once he told my mother that he felt like eating some goat's trotters (*paya*) for Sunday breakfast and she was so delighted that thereafter she would sing as she made them every other Sunday even though by the third time Papa had completely lost interest and the rest of us in the household hated the slippery, slithery feel and fatty smell of the stuff. She can still muster up a few tears every time she comes upon a well made dish of *paya*, and on the anniversary of his death often tries to take in *paya* to the mosque where such offerings are collected, prayed over and then bought for a few pounds by those unable to cook for themselves.

When he turned forty, Papa had apparently gone to the dentist and had all his teeth removed for no reason at all. He told my mother that he had read somewhere that it was a hygienic thing and that one needed to cut down on eating at this stage of one's life anyway. He found hardly anyone to sympathise with the agony that he had to live with for months afterwards, particularly as he said that he had no regrets. But I suppose for a man who believed that eating was hardly a worthwhile human activity, it was, in the end, no great loss. He did not appear to suffer any pangs of conscience either about the huge dental bill that took years to pay.

But for the eighteen months that he was a manager at the Canton Restaurant, until it went badly bust, he was the happiest I had seen him in my life. In a new suit, cigarette in his hand, chequebook in his pocket, he held the world in his hands. He wandered around the tables in the restaurant discussing politics, the end of British rule, business ventures he was going to go into next, the partition of India and Pakistan, anything that was buzzing around his feverish head which he felt obliged to share with diners whether they were interested or not. In time, inevitably, the finely dressed customers in their shimmering saris and expensive suits, often there to celebrate their wedding anniversaries (another expensive and meaningless import from England), fell away and the Canton began to attract more after City Bar eaters, all men, all voluble because drunk, all happy to listen to my father and most unable to pay for anything but promising always to settle soon.

City Bar was almost entirely responsible for the ruin of the few unreliable Asian men we had in our community. City Bar was the one place I did not visit when I went home after twenty-two years. People in the mosque were more than eager to tell me that the City Bar family was back. These days they count with great excitement every returnee who adds to their numbers and gives them the feeling that the good old days are only a few inches away. The mosque does indeed look like we never left. But a year before I visited it, they say there were goats roaming the beautiful hall with its white pillars and mosaic floor and that fierce-looking men – supporters of Idi Amin – had claimed they had the right to the place because they were Muslims. Troops stormed the mosque, men and goats were killed or ejected and the bullet and blood marks have been repaired and whitewashed. It is back to business as usual with returnees animatedly discussing where the money is to be made these days or grumbling about the state of the houses they have been handed back and idolising the newly rich. The only difference is that instead of the three thousand people who used to crowd out the place there are a few hundred, whose voices resonate around the massive empty spaces.

The City Bar family and others, those who were worth something once, are back to take up their place again. They all made more than enough money in the countries which had given them refuge, places like Canada and Britain, but that was not enough.

How peculiar is and was the morality we live(d) by. It did not matter how deeply evil we believed alcohol was, or how strictly we monitored personal behaviour, or how much we condemned malpractice or any transgression or what we gossiped about. If any of the above produced money in plenty for those responsible, these people mattered, they were revered. Or at least forgiven far too quickly. My mother, who hated the sight of that bar and all that it had meant in the early days of her married life, was close friends with the many wives of the City Bar men who all lived in a house with velvet curtains and peacock feathers in pink vases.

For a very short time, I think Papa thought he had gained that deep respectability he had pretended to scorn all his life and he understood how important this was. His voice was disdainful as he rang chacha Ramzan and Shamsu to invite them to the restaurant. Previously, his contempt for them was tinged with slight unease. It was agnosticism rather than atheism. They both came with their 'secretaries', blonde East European women with impossibly high heels and dresses ruched around their buttocks, one red, one orange. Chacha and his son talked to my father like he was one of them at last. My father bountifully gave them a free meal.

My mother was invited by Papa, not once but twice to eat downstairs and he even told her what sari he wanted her to wear. He taught her about Babycham and cognac. Although she now thinks pink bubbles would be too unsuitable for a woman of her age, hidden amongst the best saris you will always find a bottle of French cognac. ('It is good for my heart and the bones you know, only for the medicine reasons. I don't like it to drink.') Then came odd presents. A beautiful miniature, silver filigree rickshaw, ivory ornaments and just before the ignoble collapse of the enterprise, a stunning gold dragon locket for my mother. She keeps this wrapped in a silk hankie, and is still debating with herself who she should leave it to. The identity of the recipient changes every month as she makes fresh calculations not only about who in the family has been nicest and most caring towards her, but also the very complicated business of inheritance: should it go to the only son and his children or should it go to my father's favourite daughter, my sister, as a way of atoning for the terrible way he rejected her? Or is it better to leave it to the eldest grandchild who was named by my father (after his heroine Farah Diba, the wife of the ex-Shah of Iran whom my father admired as a cultured fellow) or to the youngest grandchild because she is the last of that generation?

My brother started respecting Papa again, and once, just once, borrowed money from him for petrol. Both men puffed with pride as my father dipped into his pocket.

As time went by, more and more of those who started

crowding around Papa were the hangers-on, the ones who had no intention of ever paying for the fancy dinners they brought their clients to, knowing full well that this was not a man who would keep tabs or extract a shilling. When he had his final scene with Kanti, Papa remained remorseless: 'Kanti, you stupid man, it is only money. You can't take it with you anywhere.'

The sign for the Canton Restaurant is still flapping in the dusty wind. The place now, like almost every third shop in Kampala, has been turned into a fax bureau.

I recently met an elderly businessman – a millionaire – who has returned to Uganda after years of exile in order to reclaim his property and business. He wanted to know who my father was. The name did not ring a bell. He was perplexed. I told him about my father's extraordinary lack of success when it came to business. He looked at me seriously for some time and then said: 'My dear it was very difficult not to make money here, to be a failure. Your father must have been a very special man.'

He was.

This particular failure had a much more profound effect on all our lives than anything that had gone before. For years my mother had learned to expect nothing and to laugh away her disappointments – which she could still feel – when her expectations were gratified. This time, I guess she had allowed herself to become hopeful, and to enjoy the fruits of my father's short-lived success. She was desolate. In fact bitterness was everywhere again, and this time we all knew that there were unlikely to be more comebacks or chances for any of us to break out of what was coming. I look back now and think of the way my mother wept more tears then than at any time before. She said she was crying for my father more than herself. She had seen how self-respect had transformed him into somebody tangible, worthy and real and she knew he would now sink into his own increasingly despairing and claustrophobic world.

My brother felt betrayed, I think. (And to think he was the

same age as Kanti, who simply went on to tamper around with the next bit of the family fortune.) And trapped again, the way he had been since the age of seventeen when he'd had to take his first job filling up cars in a petrol station. To fulfil his obligations, which were unique, as the only son of a failed father. I don't know if it would have been harder had he been the failed son of a successful father. What onerous expectations we have of our sons. Little wonder so many turn monstrously self-loving.

As time went on, Amir began to relish his recaptured dominance of the family and the ownership of those who depended on him. But underneath he was deeply affected; frightened at being the only one who could hold us together, unnerved by his sense of responsibility and the steady hand with which he could hold on to a job and impress his bosses. Most of all worried that this meant he could never make his own life in the future.

But he did, and with a vengeance.

I do understand how hard he worked for us and how much he must have resented it. With us hanging onto his life, he could never breeze about like all the other young men around him, their father's money tumbling out of their pockets, replenished at will. And I was grateful. But when he started demanding adulation, obedience, accolades, even the gratitude seemed to die. I know him too well to worship him the way I once did. I remember too many moments of pain and confusion and how my mother learned to tailor her words and actions to fit in with his whims and demands, to be obsequious instead of the free and proud woman who had raised us. But without him, I don't know where our vulnerable family would have ended up and how can I ever forget that?

PART 2

1961–1972

Liberation is not deliverance.

Victor Hugo,
Les Misérables

9

By the time I finished primary school, in 1961, the certainties of the fifties were disengaging themselves and life was taking other twists and turns. Out there, just as in our lives at home, we gradually became aware of nebulous shifts in this and that and an atmosphere of speechless dread was developing. We were not just getting more and more detached from black Ugandans; we began to fear them in a way we had never done before. I look back now and can see that in 1959 I knew no black people and cannot even remember the names of the servants who worked for us. In part, the Mau Mau stories helped to feed the apprehension, but I think it was also, deep down, a realisation that the past and its social order was petering out and those who knew their place were creeping (sometimes striding) out of the places allocated to them. There was more defiance in the eyes of the servants as we spoke to them, a deliberate slowing down when we told them to hurry, a swagger in their movements, with a few really impertinent ones saying things like independence was coming and our white masters would not be there long to protect us.

Suddenly other tenants in Century House started putting bars (of different designs) up on their windows. The fences and gates around the posh houses now had broken glass bottles and barbed wire for protection. More *askaris*, security men, with unfeeling eyes and long sticks, were employed to sit by the gates of those lucky enough to have gardens. More Alsatians were seen next to them. People stayed at home when dusk came in except to go to mosque or temple and pray for what we didn't even know. Out on the streets there was a silence punctuated by Kiri-Kiri music from the few African bars that were actually in the town. Bank deposit boxes began to be used. Fewer jewels were worn. Women shopping in the market lost the ease with which they would wander around mingling and haggling. Now they cast their eyes around looking for that criminal who was going to snatch their necklace or purse. Some started stuffing notes into their bras and then had to face the dilemma of how to extract the money without encouraging the (presumed) lasciviousness of the black men around.

Asians in East Africa have always created greater anxiety and fear for themselves than was ever necessary or borne out by events. At least until the expulsions by Idi Amin in Uganda. The number of Asians who have ever been killed in Uganda, Tanzania or Kenya remains astonishingly minute, if one considers the turbulent histories of those countries and the lack of awareness and sensitivity with which most of us lived our lives. Perhaps this was because we had been placed in the soft middle of two forces, because we knew we did not truly belong, that as a minority with few rights and even less real power, we were always going to be vulnerable.

But not all the fears were fantasies or a hidden yearning for the way it used to be. Many Africans were indeed covetous of the wealth of the *wahindis*, without ever understanding how hard and long people had had to work for what they had accumulated. All Asians were unfairly thought to be wealthy and avaricious; all Africans assumed to be the innocent children of the garden of Eden by those black people who had assumed power.

But in spite of these tensions and the sense that history was moving inexorably on, independence in 1961 came with a pop rather than a bang, although one did feel moved when the

Union Jack quivered painfully down the pole. The firework display however was unforgettable. Asian businessmen had backed the winning politicians and even contributed a few floats to the procession on the day: dull lorries with messages like INDEPENDENCE DAY. BEST WISHES FROM THE SUGAR WORKS GROUP. The most imaginative one had a young girl dressed as a fairy in a blonde wig waving sweetly and throwing sweets to the crowd. It took me a while to realise it was that bloody Naseem again. The usual worthy speeches were made and we all learned and sang the National Anthem:

> Oh Uganda,
> Land of Freedom
> We hold the future in our hands
> United Free
> For Liberty.

Dear, oh dear are ideals only big illusions? Over the decades of carnage that followed a few years after independence, how did poor common people in Uganda feel when they saw or heard these words?

Perhaps independence seemed to lack emotional signifi-cance because, unlike the freedom struggles in India or Kenya, there was no massive uprising, no shedding of blood, and heroes did not feature. Ordinary Ugandans then and even now are generally warm, happy and benign people, except when they encounter petty thieves who are too stupid not to get caught. That is why it has been so easy for indescribably bestial leaders and militiamen to take control over the country and bleed it till it has been all but completely sapped. The Mau Mau resistance, which was ruthless and brutal and which had inflicted terminal wounds on the power of whites in Kenya, mortified the peaceful Ugandans as much as it did the British. If there were any political protests, they tended to lack real force or commitment, like the inept swipes one makes at determined and unstoppable African flies.

This was when Papa made impressive speeches at me about how we should behave better towards the black man. This made him exceptional in my eyes, and although there were a greater number of vituperative rows about my relationship with Naseem, the stiff petticoats I wore, the Cliff Richard songs I was singing around the house and my *Bunty* comics, which he would toss around the room when he wanted to feel he was in control, he did teach me to question things the way I might never have done with a millionaire father. My mother also came into her own at this time, able to say with utter sincerity that all this money, wealth and ostentation was more headache than it was worth and that rich people had no *shanti* (peace and quiet) in their lives. Her friends like Meherunbai and Zora Masi who you felt were actually propped up by the gold on their neck, arms and ears, would nod sagely, and agree, only ever in principle of course, and pronounce her a very wise woman.

It has always intrigued me how many rich Asians have a soft spot for people like my mother, and now me, perhaps because it is boring to surround yourself with others as rich as yourself. There is also, I suspect, curiosity about those who don't share the passion for money that most of my people are born with. In the twenty-three years I have been here, I have only met four people from my community who seem not to be driven by the need to make money. Among my other acquaintances, those who have acquired wealth are excitedly hatching schemes to make more and those who haven't are working all hours to get there.

I get invited to dinner parties by those I once went to school or parties with: often people I instinctively relate to because we speak the same language and share a history, although I used to think most were so mundane and without imagination. I feel they know or have known a unique part of me – and I need them to keep those memories going. We are a people with no history, otherwise. But I also feel an alien in their midst and most of the time I am there I end up having profound conversations with the bustling thoughts in my own head, only periodically coming out of these to laugh at the same old joke with the same old person who has no idea what to say to me.

These people live in vast houses in places like Ruislip or commuter villages in Sussex with gold-framed English landscape prints on their walls and the odd painting of an Indian dancer that they picked up on their three-week luxury tour of Rajasthan: 'Great time we all had, you know, three couples, no other Indians, just Europeans, and you know continental food in the big hotels, because you know the children don't like our food and we didn't want the stomach problems.'

They feel immensely successful because now they have thousand-piece silver cutlery sets and obsequious smiling white waitresses in uniform who pass around the drinks and 'bites' at these occasions. 'Sala, when we came here, had we ever seen an English servant? Look at them now, they are serving us.' Unlike their parents, these young affluents have little real sense of compassion or respect for those not in their league, except, as in my case, as a petty distraction. But the people they despise most of all are those who allow themselves to fall from elevated positions. Suddenly the folk who were introduced to you first not by name but by their wealth – 'Have you two met? This man owns seven hotels in Vancouver and property in Dallas, you say you don't know him? *Yaar*, tell her who you are' – mysteriously disappear from the dining circles. You innocently ask, as one does, where so-and-so is these days – and after looks and smiles dart across the table, they tell you with the greatest relish how he is now bankrupt or living in a flat somewhere in Hounslow or even in prison, where some of our great and rich have found themselves after nefarious dealings with the cream of British society.

I still eke out some arrogance from the fact that these people don't read books and that they fill up the coffers of the Tory Party without the slightest understanding of politics or society. In one house, there used to be a painting of Margaret Thatcher on the main wall of the living room. In another, a picture of Idi

Amin, because he forced them to leave so they could come to this land of milk and honey.

'So tell me, how much do you make in the journalism, all this television and you know?' is a question that is always thrown in by some cigar-smoking man with a proud moustache and hands covered with curly black hair and diamonds. I do make it my business to tell them so they can fall about laughing and inform me that their secretaries earn more or that their wives spend that much in a month. They love it, baiting somebody they knew was always doing better than them in exams, now driving around in a pathetic C-registration Honda (at the last party, all the thirty cars outside were Mercedes or BMWs) and ranting on about something called socialism: 'You want to see the socialism, come with me to my factory in Russia, see those idiots, worse than the Africans.' Yes, the youngest and newest of our entrepreneurs are to be found in the Eastern bloc, cutting their teeth in the lands of nothing, transporting the good life in crates filled with chocolates, cigarettes and ties which pretend to be by some French designer, coming back with so much money they are genuinely at a loss about what to do with it so that the extent of their instant wealth can be recognised. One friend, who was the school idiot, now has a house with seven bathrooms and piped music in every one of them. Andrew Lloyd Webber songs mostly, because he takes his Russian middle-men to the shows for a treat and a bribe when he flies them over and he now knows most of the words. When drunk, where once he used to bang on the table and sing Mukesh songs – Mukesh being the playback singer in Hindi films who always sang about broken hearts and broken dreams – in a voice gurgling with tar and dragging to keep up with the melody, now we get 'Don't cry for me Miss [*sic*] Argentina.'

I love the banter too, being the radical, the outsider who knows everything better than they do, but who never seems to mint success the way they can. Another favourite topic of conversation comes up: 'You really should not be so political, just keep quiet, that is the way for us. Keep your nose clean, keep your nose out of the trouble.' Others find my outspoken views on women a 'little too much extremist. You will spoil the women. We give them everything, all this libbers and that it is nonsense. Our wives live like queens, ask them.'

Well, not quite. But in small groups, they do congregate and talk about how to spend money on marble statues at Harrods or the elevated positions they are beginning to gain in the mosque or in some safe cultural association. Their conversations are (relatively) more interesting than those of the men who spend every living moment of the day wheeling and dealing, networking with such commitment that if necessary they will even arrange to fall in love with and marry the sister or daughter of somebody they wish to nurture. The marriages last for ever.

10

Kololo Senior Secondary School – motto 'Lead Kindly Light', still to be found painstakingly embroidered on the clean white shirts worn by the black schoolchildren who now go there – was, at the time I first went there, entirely Asian. The classrooms were a row of wooden huts, painted grey with tin roofs that made such a racket when it rained that most teachers had to stop and give us writing to do. We used the time more profitably laughing and chatting to each other and no amount of bellowing from the teachers really reached us in any serious way.

There was a square where we had morning assembly and thirty-five wide high steps which led to the headmaster's office and the staffroom. They were thirty-five tremblingly terrifying steps for those who were called up for a beating for any misdemeanour. And they were a glorious ascent for those who were called upon to read the prayers and read out incomprehensible but worthy platitudes like 'To be a servant is better than to be a cheat' written by Mr Patel, the headmaster.

He was a seriously violent man, with pale skin and eyes that were almost totally covered up by flappy eyelids until he opened them to pin you with a glare and a gleam like a horribly sadistic Dickensian figure in charge of powerless orphans. This happened when he was announcing some terrible punishment for one or all of us. He had an arm that could drive a cane to make any leg bleed in five minutes and most horrifying of all, a huge, partially toothless mouth that was black and orange because he chewed betel-nut all day. His room was always deadly dark and smelt of pain. When he shouted, droplets would accompany his virulent words like spitting venom. The only time one saw another side to this man was when we had our annual day celebrations and some condescending minor white civil servant – and in later years a self-important black politician checking that Asians were being suitably obsequious in recognition of his status and their past arrogance – was invited as the guest of honour. Most of the African dignitaries were slimy, self-serving creatures, open to persuasion and veneration as long as your overtures were accompanied by some luxury or (preferably) money.

On these occasions, Mr Patel would clench his hands, smile continuously, even at pupils, and bow so low that at times and from a distance you could only see his hunchback. In his speech he would thank God for allowing him to serve the next generation and to enable them to 'blossom like roses of the future'. He would grasp our hands fiercely with emotion as he gave us our school prizes.

In an odd sort of way he did care. When I got extraordinarily good A-level results, he spent his own money to present me with a 22-carat-gold medal engraved with our motto. My teenage son fell about with embarrassment and laughter when I showed it to him the other day.

Everyone feared him: his teachers, his pupils and all our parents. Even occasionally my mother, though she soon found a way to make him smile at her. Fear of him drove us to succeed and many of us today feel a sad sense of loss as our children go through their education with soft, gentle headmasters too ready to understand and even anxious to be seen to be matey with our terrible adolescents.

When boys started appearing in school with a sort of Beatles haircut, he would pin their hair back with hairpins and parade them as degenerates during assembly. Then he decided that girls with fringes were also trying to look like the Beatles and started snipping any hair that lay across the forehead. This led to a particularly troubled phase of my life. I was born with one of those enormous foreheads which kind people said meant I was brainy. Teenage hormones had inflicted what we used to call pimples on this embarrassing feature. It was only by having a long thick fringe that I could hide both these blemishes – although this did in fact encourage even more crops of spots, breeding under perfect conditions of darkness, airlessness and with the nutrients provided by greasy hair. When Patel started going for the girls with his scissors, I would wretchedly hide in the classroom through every break, or put my head down on the desk pretending to have a headache.

Thank God it was a passing phase. Soon his anger was turned on those girls who had started backcombing their hair and using hairspray. He would force them to comb their hair out with a broken comb he had kept for the purpose. The girls would weep with shame and pain as the tangles were pulled out and while he was screaming at them: 'Stupid girls, no culture, no manners, just shameless, disgrace to the school and your parents. I will sort you out, put your eyes down at once.'

Mrs Bose was another tyrant. She saw wantonness and dissolution everywhere. A ponderous woman, fat and with no sign of a neck, looking like a large turtle who had been upon the earth for ever, always dressed in a white sari and brown lace-up men's shoes, she would shuffle around looking for what she called 'sinful' girls who 'will get pregnant before they pass their Cambridge'. Her rules, which came and went at random, were even more bizarre. Girls with long plaits had to wear thick petticoats under their shirts and make sure that the plaits were always behind. This was so that the grease from the hair which was always well oiled could not soak into the shirt and reveal the bra straps which would turn the boys mad with desire and presumably end up in this pregnancy before we got to take our O levels. She would not however agree to instruct our mothers not to oil our hair, which left us smelling of stale coconuts, mustard and rose essence. This is what we all wanted. But Bose rightly calculated that the risks of unbridled passion would increase hugely if boys could lay their hands on soft wavy locks instead of the offputtingly tight and sticky plaits so many of us had. Bose also loved to wield scissors, usually to snip open the hem of our skirts if she deemed them to be too short. The next day the hems were up again. Such defiance.

One day she interrupted our geography lesson, told B. K. Amin our elfin teacher to sit in the corner and then triumphantly brought out a newspaper cutting. It was a story about a clockmaker, an Asian man who was known to be of flaccid morals and who it was rumoured had sex with African women from the Hi-Life Club. 'Finally, he has met his punishment,' announced Mrs Bose. He had been making love to his assistant in his shop the night before and had got stuck inside her vagina. Word had spread as daylight came and thousands had gathered outside the shop to cheer and jeer. Police had to come and rescue the exhausted couple. The journalist claimed they had sawn off the clockmaker's most essential part and that there would no longer be any more 'tick tock, tick tock in his life'. Mrs Bose was looking very sombre at the end of the story. When we burst out laughing, she said: 'You are just the immodest children. Beware of the sex things, you can see the troubles it can make. You have the Cambridge in a few years. Girls, protect your shame. Boys, remember the clockmaker.' Mrs Bose would not have impressed judges at any English elocution competitions, but she was a matchless maths and science teacher, as were so many of our other teachers imported from India at this time. Local Asians were not prepared to go into teaching because the pay was so low.

Many of those who came over to teach were excellent teachers, but we foolishly made fun of them especially those who were too unsure of themselves to control us. East African Asians by this time had persuaded themselves that they were superior to those who had not left the subcontinent. We spoke English with a better accent, we had been colonised for much longer, we were therefore better. In many ways these memories show much more our inclination to caricature people we did not respect than what the teachers were really like.

There was the poor B. K. Amin, small, bald and with eyes that were glazed with fear. He spent the first three minutes of every lesson wiping his chair and then his hands. He repeated the entire performance when he had written anything on the blackboard with chalk. His fear turned to panic when it rained and apoplexy when there was any lightning or thunder. We always knew when he was unable to cope, because he would repeat the same sentence over and over again in an ever-weakening voice. We made a fool of the poor man, little realising that he had been traumatised during the war when he had been bombed on a battleship in Burma. On a good day, he could become quite assertive and sanguine. 'Stand up Yasmin, girl, stand up madam. Look at your life and ponder, girl. You can be a star, like the stars in the sky, but girl, you must apply yourself with seriousness, with dedication. And you, Hussain, do you know how hard your father and grandfather work for you? Blood, tears, and sweating. Repay them my boy, work hard, shine, hold their heads up. Good blood must show.'

And I paid him back by laughing mercilessly at him and jumping out of the windows when he wasn't looking, and then coming back into the class. Especially when it was raining. Oh, we all did laugh so.

Mr Ravi was another favourite. Our history teacher. His sympathy was always with the British. What he wanted more than anything else was to give India back to those 'born to rule, those who know how to rule because it is in their veins, in the way they walk'. He would march, stride around the class singing: 'Sons of France, Come listen to the Duke of Burgundy.' Is there, was there ever such a song? He had us clapping and saluting the Union Jack when the British put down the Indian mutiny. I still have not forgiven him for that. His grasp of history was beautifully simple and lucid. The Tsar warned those who opposed him: 'Do not do mischief in my kingdom.' And the French Revolution was caused by 'misbehaved peasants who did not have the education'.

Mr Ravi looked impoverished and undernourished. He wore the same two shirts every other day, and a jacket with so many leather patches that it would have looked quite fashionable in the seventies. There was always a much-loved, much-used book in one of the collapsing pockets. He was thin, tall though stooped, and had a face which had a thousand years etched upon it. Perhaps it was because he was a man with many many children, who appeared to have not even a year between them. The eldest child had a name which began with an 'A', Aruna, and the rest ran down the alphabet until we reached Hatish. When we had our annual celebrations at the school, he would walk them all down the hill, carrying their shoes in a big bag. Mrs Ravi would struggle somewhere behind the long line, in her crumpled cotton sari and thin hair twisted into a half-hearted bun into which she had stuck a flower. At the school gates they would all put on their shoes and within minutes you would see bleeding knees as they tried and failed to run in shoes they were completely unused to wearing. The story was that each year the one with the largest feet got a new pair of shoes and all the others were passed down. The last pair was kept for the time they could send them off to their even poorer relatives in India. A few hours later, Mrs Ravi would be smearing black boot polish from her bag on to the shoe bites that most of her children by then would be complaining of, muttering to whoever was nearby about how miraculously the polish worked.

Mr Bhonsle was given the task of teaching us English and physics. A man of strange logic and linguistic abilities, he would say confusing things like: 'We need two projectors, therefore we have none', or 'Sit two each on one chair.'

He developed two personalities for the two subjects he taught us. The physics teacher was dry, stern, stiff, silent and sneering, walking by the rows of pupils, most of whom understood nothing at all about the subject and knowing that they would find abuse and not enlightenment in the many hours they were scheduled to pass with Bhonsle. What terrorised us most was the fact that he could remain so silent for so long, only interrupting the silence with loud barks if somebody was fidgeting or in order to pronounce us all idiots.

But Bhonsle, the literature teacher was completely different. Too many words, too big for his mouth rolling around, swilling around and pouring forth in a gush which though jumbled was deeply felt. He gesticulated, climbed on chairs, spoke from the furthest corners of the rooms where birds were nesting and where the mice loved to hide. The creatures would scurry with some irritation as he held forth, unstintingly passionate, undaunted by the persistent problems he had with the long vowel sound.

During these lessons, he didn't care whether we giggled or not. He was in his own world and we were there, mere spectators, privileged menials. Proverbs were another favourite of his and these we were forced to write out in our little book and learn by heart. When he got them wrong, we learned them wrong and these were mistakes that have proved to be impossible to correct over the years. I still say 'Thrice bitten, twice shy' even though my English friends insist that thrice is an archaic word in their language.

Of course it was easy to deride these teachers and it is even easier now, when so many of us can use a fish fork and speak with an (almost) pukka accent. But this is a tribute to them, those men and women, underpaid but deeply revered because they were teachers, who more than anything else taught us the value of learning and discipline. Taught us too that the world would never be quite the way we wanted it to be, that hopes would need to accommodate reality and that success was bound up with knowing the limits of rebellion and the benefits of living within some moral boundaries. Through fear, forced rote learning, mercilessly being pushed, we passed our exams and all round the world, outstanding lawyers, scientists, doctors, businessmen and politicians relate to their children how these teachers at a nondescript school moulded their ambitions and abilities. Their good words stayed with us, the wisdom they imparted informs the way we live our lives and I grew to love Shakespeare's words because I first learned to laugh at them.

One day Patel decided that too much Westernisation was creeping into our lives and that the way to halt this was to import his best friend Chottabhai (his name meant 'Shortie') from India and introduce compulsory music and dance lessons for all of us. Chottabhai arrived in his white *kurta* and pyjamas, a basketful of *gungrus* (heavy ankle bells), tablas and a beautiful sitar in a silk bag which he pulled along on a makeshift trolley. The only place Patel could find for him to inject old world culture into us was on a small concrete slab – another unfinished building – near the canteen and opposite the cage which held Moti, the monkey, our school pet. Brought in and loved to pieces by Bhonsle.

Moti, whose life had been full of boredom, the unfeeling harassment of schoolkids, and an unsuitable diet (we gave him all the food we didn't want to eat at lunchtime and he was often found groaning in his cage suffering from gut-ache) became insufferably happy and loud, encouraged by the music and dancing girls. Chottabhai went into a trance as soon as he started playing and singing, but even with his eyes closed he knew exactly who was going out of step. Patel was right. The music did echo in our souls, awakening some ancient ancestral connections although none of us had ever been exposed to classical Indian music before. He started teaching us Bharatna-tyam dancing. He never moved from his two cushions on the floor but we did learn at least the first steps, just by following his very precise instructions. For a short time we began to weave flower garlands through our plaits and wear glass bangles, which would shatter at any excuse, and discuss the greatness of Ravi Shankar. We scorned all those girls we deemed shallow because they did not embrace their Indian heritage and sang only filmy tunes. The phase did not last long.

Ruhi, Bhonsle's daughter, a big-boned awkward girl, turned out to be an unexpectedly talented dancer but Chottabhai soon stopped patting her on the back and beaming every time he was talking about her. This was because she decided that she wanted to go into Hindi films (where all dancers were courtesans, albeit some as a result of desperate need or terrible coercion). Soon instead of the aesthetic quality of her movements, she was concentrating on creating a range of inviting looks (frolicking eyebrows, flashing, fluttering, winking eyes, now sullen, now sad, now delighted, now sexy) and pouting lips which would silently mouth flirtatious Hindi songs. Chottabhai, with his eyes closed, was unaware of any of this until he heard Patel, who had come to watch us practising, bellowing almost into his ear one day. With the approval of her father, Ruhi got three strokes of the cane on her hands. A few months later she was sent off to India, and the last I heard of her she had been seen as a chorus girl in a Raj Kapoor film. Rumour has it that she's had an illegitimate child with some male actor.

The week following her disgrace, Mohammed, a young Muslim boy, who loved watching Ruhi dance, stole the monkey but made it seem like the animal had escaped. Bhonsle shook with grief and anxiety. Patel ordered Ravi and B. K. to climb the trees and use his binoculars to look around the garden trees to find him. B. K. was even more frightened of saying no to Patel than of climbing trees, although he declined the binoculars and spent the time clutching the trunk like an inexperienced bush-baby. Ravi used the occasion to shout forth adages like: 'A hero is a man who does what he can', and singing 'Rule Britannia'.

Mohammed brought the monkey back after a week, when despair had set in and hope had fled from Mr Bhonsle's face. Moti had been kept in the toilet of the petrol station owned by Mohammed's father and he had nearly torn the place down.

But being an only and hugely spoilt son, Mohammed got away with things the rest of us would have been killed for. He also had cheek. He said he had found the animal and was pronounced boy of the week during assembly.

Life was transforming irreversibly now. By 1965 the country had been independent for three years, but real change had had to wait in the wings. There was impatience in the air, a gathering momentum. The Asians, however, remained self-absorbed, peering intently into their own lives, like a half-blind man reading a small-print book, never looking up and blinking unseeingly when the light invades.

Whenever they felt a twinge of official disapproval, or heard political leaders talking about Africanisation, a rush of alarm moved swiftly through the community. For the first time people started to understand what had happened to them historically and were forced to confront the consequences of never having developed a political base or even sense. Here they were, no longer tied in any meaningful way to the subcontinent; most families had now been in Uganda for generations, all loved (and continue to love) the country deeply. Many felt betrayed, first by the British for their withdrawal and then by the blacks who never did acknowledge what they gave to the place and instead maligned them for doing what human beings do – looking after their own economic interests.

These were justifiable arguments. After all, in the many years since independence, the black elite has behaved with greater greed, cruelty and absence of conscience than Asians ever did. And if it hadn't been for the Asians, the vital commercial infrastructure would simply not have existed. As Sophie, my black Ugandan friend whose husband and father were killed by the military and whose only daughter died of AIDS said the other day over a drink: 'Yasmin, don't be so hard on your people. We are so good, in fact excellent, at destroying ourselves too. All that killing that happened when you all left, whose fault was that? At least when you were there we could

110

buy bandages and soap to wash off the blood with good soap powder!' Loud, bitter laughter.

Almost all doctors, lawyers, pharmacists and accountants were Asian. Most honestly believed they had a right to be there for ever and many proved this allegiance by taking on Ugandan passports when they had a choice. Papa began to believe he had a messianic purpose, grabbing hold of anybody polite enough to stop and listen, telling them not to give him their most priceless possession, their British passport even if it was only a grade D and meant nothing in real terms. Soon, people started scurrying off before he had reached them, pretending not to hear him shouting their names. 'Stupids they are, just stupids. Giving up a British passport, the best passport in the world, what is there to choose? They will send gunboats to save us anywhere in the world, the British will, nobody can dare to touch a British subject. Get your bloody Ugandan passports, you will remember my words one day.' He got himself a safe deposit box in the Bank of India and locked away our blue 'For God and the Queen' passports. He died before he was forced to see how abject we were to become because it was the colour of our skins and not the blue of the passports we were clutching that mattered.

11

But even as Asians were asserting their faith in the country, many were feeling a deep despondency. Dobabhai, the school administrator, started writing sad symbolic poetry about unrequited love and in the eyes of the older men there was a fading of light and hope and the confidence they once used to carry. Pain too that their contribution, their role, was barely being recognised in the rush to demolish the past and to cast them as villains.

Sensing their vulnerability and lack of protection, Africans who knew their time was coming started provoking and insulting those they felt were easiest to terrify. An old man walking with his daughter and someone would shout, 'Hey Mzee, old man, let me marry your daughter, or let me take her to my bed. I have never had a *wahindi* before.' Others would deliberately bump into you or trip you up and then roar with laughter. Asians would remain silent but inside they were trembling with apprehension and rage. They knew that even if they were attacked the police who were all black were unlikely to do anything to protect people who were weak and unwanted by the majority.

If you went to the post office to pay your bills, to get your visas, you learned to expect that indignity was part of the course. The officials would look at you languidly, keep talking to each other in local languages which you did not understand, sometimes deliberately allow time to pass until it was too late.

These people despised us so much that they weren't even interested in our bribes.

This kind of abusive behaviour got significantly worse when African politicians began to realise that the 'honourable' British government didn't want the *wahindis* either. The officials in the British High Commission were equally uncivil to the hordes of desperate people trying to leave and get into Britain as hysteria grew in Britain and laws began to be passed which made it impossible for Asian British passport holders to come freely into the motherland. It is hard to describe the atmosphere of that time. The sense of insecurity, of being despised, of losing respect and position, of watching the whole world that you had known and in part created dissolve into vapours of venom and nothingness. Even Ramzan chacha was afraid: 'What does all this money mean now? These houses, shops, our gold? These *shenzis* will take it all and what will they do with it?' My mother pretended to agree with him: 'Yes, life is so temporary we come into this world naked and we take nothing when we die. So why worry about things so much?'

And thus it was in all households. Homespun philosophy, politics, ethics, faith, and money of course, being despondently discussed in every veranda as the sun set and dusk came in and before those who went to mosque had to go in for their baths. Attendance at the morning prayers – at four o'clock in the morning – which previously would have consisted of maybe fifty people rose to a thousand, although most families were now escorted by their sleepy *askaris* who had to sit patiently outside in the mist and the cold while their masters and mistresses desperately prayed for the world not to change.

One of the terrible things about injustice is the way it poisons any future possibilities because revenge has to have its day in the meantime. It also poisons perceptions so that you only ever see vengeance or the mirror image of your own behaviour in those you once wronged and believe these to be the only possible explanations for their actions.

So when we simply saw greater assertiveness among blacks –

something that was inevitable and long overdue – the sense of doom in our hearts grew and we hated it. Black people now walked and talked differently. They dared to say things about unfairness, in bars, in our own kitchens, in the streets. Their nerve unnerved us and we complained to each other about it. The turnover of servants accelerated. Zora Masi went with her driver, frantically looking for new servants every few weeks. The driver left after a few months with the lovely new ayah who was expecting their child. There were now looks of anger when swish cars drove by splashing those who sold things on the pavements. Even Kanti had to hold his tongue and keep his head down. Where once the people might have laughed or cursed imperceptively, they would now shout, and the force of their voices came from their growing revulsion at the sight of the emblems of affluence and those who flaunted them.

It worked the other way round too. When Africans saw real generosity or the desire to alter the way we related to them, they read it cynically as one more example of the *wahindi*'s cunning.

Maybe we were simply incapable of comprehending the implications of the ominous changes around us. That's what my father said. That we still thought like the dukawallah, without foresight, without an understanding of the place and the time we were so busy minting money in. I don't think he was right. I think people did see only too clearly what was happening and that the realisation paralysed them.

There were exceptions but we did not really rate these people. When an Asian man became an MP in the independent Uganda – and that was truly a remarkable event – the talk was all about how useful he was going to be to Asians when they needed to bypass regulations or 'reward' the right person. When Sugra Visram, an outstanding Asian woman, who, with the approval of her husband, stood in the first post-independence election and was elected by a huge majority of black women to parliament, my people could only question her motives and disapprove of her unconventional rise to prominence. They gossiped endlessly and mercilessly about how she

115

might have got there, how her mixing with the Africans and her friendship with the Bagandan king, the Kabaka was somehow improper, how this sort of thing was corrupting the purity which all Asian women were presumed to have.

Sugra Visram, married to a descendant of the great pioneer Allidina Visram, the man who opened up the great trade routes into the interior, flourished in the knowledge that she was a cut above the rest of us for reasons which were too sophisticated for us to understand. Exquisitely beautiful and intelligent, she was certainly never going to spend her life in the narrow if comfortable space allotted to her by society. Predictably she was my mother's friend, another misfit who commanded respect by being different and in the end got it. She once proudly showed me a photograph of herself dressed in a *busuti*, a Bagandan dress with a Victorian bustle (something that came to Uganda with the missionaries and still seen all over the country) dancing with the Kabaka, her husband looking on, and it was a shock. I never saw any such thing in my childhood and I don't think it would be possible to see it today, so deep is the prejudice against black people that we have imbibed through the ages and so deep the feelings of most East Africans that this would be too audacious even to contemplate.

There is no doubt that much of this was the fault of the British, who had taught us to despise one another so that we would never properly fight them. But how long can we use that as an excuse? You cannot blame your parents for ever. Too few of us have ever confronted our own prejudices. Even among the people who have returned after so many years of exile, you find some behaving with even greater arrogance than before, boasting about how the country would not survive without them.

As the sixties moved more stridently into our lives, we were conscious that we were changing in many other ways too. No longer boring conformists like our older siblings we were learning to take risks, to act out fantasies. We had a gang, and we modelled ourselves on the schoolgirls in *Bunty*. I had also decided that I was really very much like Jo in *Little Women*. Later I became more self-confident and self-deluding, imagining that the women I had most in common with included Desdemona, Juliet and Shaw's Cleopatra.

The gang consisted of Lily, my Sindhi friend with the Kraft cheese sandwiches, named after the midwife who delivered her, Vira, the Parsee girl, and Sneh who came from a strict Punjabi family and who had been taught that respectable girls did not smile too broadly or talk too much. She adored our audacity and we liked that, so she was allowed to be in our group. We decided that it was time to ostracise Naseem because she was far too sweet and endearing to the teachers, who never saw the sharp teeth beneath her dimpled smiles. We formed a secret society, wrote out the constitution, full of spite and concocted hate, refused to speak to Naseem, shared giggles and glances when she made a mistake. I still pretended at home that she was one of my best friends because I did not want my father to feel he had won the continuing battle between us about respectable girls. Our gang was feared and admired throughout the school until the day Patel found a copy of our constitution and displayed it during the assembly.

He could not make out all our names, written in esoteric letters in blood-red ink, but he thundered nevertheless, issuing such threats that I felt a trickle of warm liquid down my legs. I moved some soil over the damp patch as we left and made sure that nobody knew about *that* disgrace. There was nowhere to hide our other dishonour. The children knew who was responsible and we knew that, the way our world was run, they would gain more respect by telling on us than by showing solidarity. Sneaks, swots and teachers' pets were feared and admired back home. Suddenly we weren't the cool cats any more. Kids avoided us, and inched their desks away from us. The worst thing was the deft way Naseem played the victim while gloating at the same time.

The schoolteachers who had made a guess as to who was involved, were outraged and deeply disappointed. They took moral education very seriously indeed and here was an example of some of the brightest girls in the school turning deliberately vindictive and cruel. Every opportunity was seized upon for the rest of that year by all the teachers either to put us down or (more effectively) to make us feel like low life who did not deserve to be near caring, sharing human beings any more. Bose would shout at us as we were gathered in a corner in the playground: 'What are you doing, you stupid girls? Making another enemy? Sit down and read Gandhiji.' Bhonsle would make me sit with him. Deshu, the short-legged maths teacher we used to call daddy-long-legs who had found the paper in the first place, called us 'devilish'. No concessions were made to the fact that we were teenagers. On the contrary. For people in our community crossing the threshold of twelve meant we were nearly grown-ups with adult responsibilities and fewer excuses.

This dishonour followed us for months. And there was another weapon that was far more unnerving. The school had not informed our parents because they still did not know who exactly were the gang leaders in this escapade. I knew that if my mother ever found out that there was the slightest whiff of a scandal or even disapproval of me by any of my teachers, she would go for me with all her emotional might. I wasn't scared of her anger, although she could slap my cheek so hard that it hurt for a good hour afterwards. I was afraid of her pain, and the agonising thought of adding another problem to her life.

Did I repent or regret what I had done to Naseem? No, not at all. She was a sweetly spiteful girl and I had no reason to feel sorry for her or for what we had done. I have never found it easy to take on the Christian virtues of repentance and forgiveness. For years she had tormented me with her beauty and I had kept her in her place by asserting myself as her intellectual superior. To make it worse, her mother let her shave her legs when we were thirteen while mine took the view that if I did this I would end up with legs as coarse as my cousin Shamsu's face, which had stubble that he could play a tune on using a small piece of cardboard. So I had dark long hair on my legs and hers looked like the Immac advert.

It was only when my friend Nazira gave me diamond-patterned stockings that I felt able to walk out with confidence again. Hot and sticky but happy. I did not have suspenders, so I tied elastic across the top of my thighs, which left sores and nearly cut off the blood supply to my legs. Or that is what it felt like, but it didn't matter.

When I turned fifteen I decided to take control by shaving my legs and armpits and putting up with the tenacious wrath of my mother. Even now, if she notices my legs which, unless I am diligent, these days can get to look very unpleasant with stiff dark hairs that stand up in the cold, she will begin a lecture on how I deliberately made hair grow on my legs by shaving them: 'You know Yassi, she never listens.' Then she whips up her sari and reveals her own smooth, ivory legs to show what might have been. Never accepting that my legs, like so much else I appear to have inherited, came from my father.

I love the pride my mother still takes in the beauty of her legs. And her hunger for life; her animated discussions about the homeless, the hounding of Neil Kinnock and the tempestuous stories by Barbara Taylor Bradford she loves to read. But most of all she is excited by the latest beauty tip she picks up and eagerly passes on to me. She has some suggestions for Bob Geldof whose picture is stuck up by the 'Home Sweet Home' poem and the silk wall hanging of Mecca, together with a picture of the Aga Khan, each deeply loved for different reasons.

Three days after she was attacked with stones by some white teenage boys outside Woolworth's in Ealing one Christmas, my mother went into a shop to buy my niece a record and got two skinheads to help her make the right choice. She bought them chocolates for their trouble. She wanted to buy them beer, but didn't know how, and anyway she has always believed that beer is elephant piss because in Uganda the popular beer had a picture of an elephant on the label. They followed her, found out where she lived and sent her a card signed: 'Happy chrismass [sic] from the lads in the record shop'.

I wish I was as noble as my mother. In 1966 I read *The*

Crucible by Arthur Miller and started calling Naseem 'Abigail' after the evil young girl in the play.

Miss Laclan arrived in the same year, the first white teacher we had ever had. We had been told she was coming weeks in advance. A French teacher from Paris: we imagined what she would be like. All swishy and wearing fragrance, just like Rita Hayworth. I knew all about Rita Hayworth because Prince Aly Khan, the son of the Aga Khan, had married her in the fifties and my mother had collected their pictures for a few years: 'See, their daughter was also called Yasmin, it is a lucky name we gave you.' The fact that almost an entire generation of girls from our community was also called Yasmin and for the same reason, and that our lives had nothing in common, made this unimpressive.

Miss Laclan was a neurotic woman in her thirties who always wore her dresses with the darts at the back, zips and buttons and a black bow pinned on the front. She walked as if she wanted to crush her feet and uncomplaining shoes into the ground. She brought her cat into the class, stroking and kissing it, and we all had to look away because we thought we would throw up – animals had their place in Africa and it was not on the lap of a lady with her lips on their heads. She was (so the gossip went) suffering from an unmendable broken heart and had come to Africa to do good. She taught us plaintive verses like: 'Il pleure dans ma coeur comme il pleure dans la ville; qui est cette langueur qui pénétre mon coeur?' She taught us nothing else that I can or could remember. If we said we did not understand her speedy ramblings she screamed at us in French and then stormed out with tears in her eyes, shaking with pain. So we did not ask any more. Most of the time she faced the board and spoke to it. We all failed our French O levels and our parents blamed us entirely, saying things like: 'You were so lucky, you had a European teacher and still you failed.' The difference between our other teachers and Miss Laclan was that for all their quirks which were too easy to laugh at, they could and did teach as if their lives depended on us doing well.

12

It was as if a floodgate had opened up. Suddenly in the sixties, Kololo School began to attract white teachers as if it were an ashram. Mr Jim Barrow, an American draft dodger, had us all drooling because he was so tall and muscular – especially when he told us that he had been one of the divers in *Dr No*. Hard to prove this either way, of course. Miss Mary, the Anglo-Indian domestic science teacher, immediately decided that being unmarried at twenty-eight and having done her cookery course in England, she had first claim to Mr Barrow. He was not choosy and allowed himself to be cooked for and cuddled by this very insecure woman who suddenly started dyeing her hair orange, perming it and looking ridiculous. She no longer wore her crucifix and the rosary she hung on her key chain was replaced by a small fading picture of Elvis in his army uniform. Smitten with all things American she was, as she had once been about all things English. She had taught us all to love and persevere with embroidery patterns of English gardens and girls wearing bonnets.

Barrow, with his sexy smile and black open-topped sports car, changed all that. For a few months, until he broke her heart by moving on to a much more sexually exciting black dancer in the local nightclub, Mary was a happy woman. She would tie her scarf tight under her chin, get into his car and be driven off at great speed at four o'clock. We would pretend to be scandalised at her shamelessness but we were madly jealous.

All the parents detested Miss Mary. She was forever teaching us to cook dishes that required expensive ingredients and were inedible. Scotch eggs, for example. Or canapés, which were all soggy by the time we had carried them home. 'What is this, dolls' food? Nothing food, like eating the air, but not free,' Vira's father would say and then, being a kind man, would force himself to eat the titbits so that his daughter did not feel a failure. The baking was more fun, and to this day most of us can make an enviably light Victoria sponge, crisp shortbread and even puff pastry.

Soon the better recipes were appropriated by our mothers and incorporated into their cooking.

The annual cookery competition at the Indian Women's Association produced dishes like saffron cake, curry puffs, shortbread with cardamom, fish marinated in coriander and then fried in butter with masala chips, a version of shepherd's pie with spicy mince. Anything which had a touch of Englishness about it won an award because it was automatically assumed that the food was healthier and better for you. The only contribution that the Indian ladies felt they were making was to the taste, which helped to make this 'healthy' food more palatable. For some years the Ismaili Women's Committee had been trying to get mothers to stop feeding their children traditional food and to move to 'proper' baby food. Suddenly Heinz never had it so good, and those who could not afford jars felt deeply ashamed and even anxious that they were depriving their beloved children. Especially when their babies did not win the annual baby competition. The fattest and whitest baby always won first prize, usually several tins of Cow & Gate powdered milk and a smocked baby dress, blue for a boy and pink for a girl, with a card with a drawing of a pink baby which said things like:

There is nothing like a baby,

122

To make the world seem brighter,
There's nothing like a baby,
To bring to the heart some laughter.

Parents would have these framed together with a picture of their baby.

Although there was no snob value to be gained by assimilating African food, in spite of ourselves we did begin to cook with *matoke*, the savoury green bananas that form the staple diet of Ugandan Africans, (*mogo*) cassava and (*karanga*) peanuts. Like the middle classes everywhere, this was part of the ever-extending greed for variety in our lives. For the poor African children, this same food caused distended bellies — something Miss Mary sounded very cross about when she was talking to us about nutrition: 'These children need a balanced diet and the parents simply don't understand this.' Yes, quite.

When we came to Britain, what we wanted more than anything else was *matoke*, *mogo* and mangoes, whatever the cost. Increasing affluence means that now we can have it all in London or Leicester, and this not only feeds our nostalgia, it reassures us that we have made it.

The other day I met an old teacher of mine who is suffering from acute depression and among other things talks incessantly about those poor African children and how, if he had it, he would leave all his money to them. He says his own belly aches when he realises that it was only when the *sanene*, the green locusts swarmed the towns, twice a year, that those children had any protein. Tears well up in his eyes as he recalls the hundreds of Africans rushing up and down the well lit streets with sheets, grabbing at the millions of insects which sometimes made it impossible to see through the windscreen: 'Once I nearly killed a boy,' he says, contrition spreading across his contorted face. 'He just ran in front of the Peugeot and I broke his leg and arm. I took him to the Mulago Hospital and gave them money.'

Actually this biannual event was not at all morbid. When the *sanene* came, it is true people went wild to eat them, but it was simply carnival time with loud dancing and singing, exciting chases, heady encounters over whose patch it was and the final triumph over these hapless insects who were transported into the other world even before they had stopped fluttering. The real connoisseurs simply broke off the legs and heads and ate them. Others crammed them into pillowcases, took them home and fried them, selling the surplus in the market the next day. A few poor Asians would buy them and then make them into a dry curry claiming that they tasted just like small chickens' legs. I was petrified of *sanene*, because they fell into your lap, on your head and into your food.

Mohammed used to stuff them into the back of my school shirt and enjoy my screams until I managed to untuck my shirt to release the creatures. Once the force of my panicky gestures killed one right against the flesh of my back. I howled for an hour as I came to terms with the sticky substance that had oozed out.

One day a large, no-nonsense Scottish woman wearing thick pink support tights and a cardigan came to address the school assembly. Her name was Miss Garvey. She towered over all the teachers there and spoke in a deep manly voice. She gained immediate respect on account of this. Unsmiling (the early missionaries never smiled either, if the drawings we had in our history books were to be believed) but empathetic, and deeply conscious of her vocation, she had come to tell us all about Girl Guides. It sounded wonderful, but I could not join.

Mainly because Amir dismissed the idea: 'You must be joking, do you think I am made of money? Do you know how much you are costing me already?' I begged. Mummy told me not to beg, that she would find the money somehow. He shouted at her and told her to stop spoiling me. We both cried because we knew that was that. Unfairly we blamed his new girlfriend, mainly because when she had first come to meet us, in her tight satin dress printed with jumbo scarlet roses and with an enormous bow tied around her conspicious hips, she had only pretended to smile. Her eyes roamed around the room as if she was surveying her territory. She did not even look at my mother when she offered her tea. My normally proud mother continued trying to tempt her with the snacks she had made, in a voice which got smaller and more servile every minute. When she left, relief and anxiety swept through the house. We prayed she wouldn't be the one he settled for. She was.

It was not a good beginning but in the end I taught myself not to care.

My mother is more forgiving these days than I am able to be. Happy too when my sister-in-law has been warm to her or taken her to mosque – she too has mellowed. I am very grateful for that because it gives my mother just enough to believe that at the end of the long journey the two of them have travelled there is some coming together. I want her to die feeling that it is all fine, that all that bitterness from the past has been laid to rest.

I know I should try to reach out too. But I am too vindictive, too angry, too sore. Happy too with my freedom from the pressure to pretend and from that weight of obligation.

Back then I was able to find consolation elsewhere. Miss Garvey also decided to start a youth club at All Saints' Church on top of the hill. She spoke to our parents, convincing them that if they did not want their children turning to sex, drugs and rock 'n' roll, they should encourage more wholesome activities. 'They are teenagers, your children. They need something to control their chemicals, otherwise they will go wild.' This was all translated into Gujarati and Hindi by Mr Ravi, who did not know the word for 'teenager'. Our parents were confused but convinced, especially when Miss Garvey said that they didn't need to pay anything for the club, only a few cents for the milk and biscuits and that although it was in a church hall, their children would not be forced to become Christians, but they should know that it was surely the most compassionate religion in the world and people in Africa and even India were converting in their thousands.

We met, we sang songs about the American railways and red red roses and, most delightful of all, we learned Scottish dancing. Miss Garvey never learned our names, so we were always given numbers as we came in, to pin to our shirts. When we weren't dancing, boys and girls sat on opposite sides of the hall, at first only tentatively crossing this great divide, but in time rushing across to grab the best dancers.

The first time we did the eightsome reel, my hands sweated as they touched the hands of a boy for the first time in my life. They sweated again in exactly the same way recently when at the age of forty-five I started going to some jiving classes and ended up with a partner called Angel. He is Spanish, a factory worker in London ('I make the stocks for the guns') who has blackened nails, expressionless eyes and grim determination to get through the music faster than anybody else. I think I sweat because I feel like a butterfly in his clasp and have this terror that without slippery hands I will be trapped for ever, just like the heroine in *The Collector*.

Quite the opposite reasons really to why I wet my hands at the youth club. By the end of the year, not only were we leaping around to near perfection, but we had learned the delights of letting our (now dry) hands linger a little in the hands of the boy we had selected to be our partner and sometimes even gathering up the courage to squeeze it a little. Going home, we would stare at the array of stars and ponder loudly about the mysteries of the galaxy.

Then I fell in love. I was fourteen. He was sixteen. I was an Ismaili, he a Hindu from a group so devoted to vegetarianism that they did not even eat root vegetables, in case insects got killed when they were pulled up. In India, I was astonished to discover, his lot went about with muslin over their noses so that small insects and even microbes were protected from the murderous inhalations of human beings. None of this made any sense to him, though. He was determined to escape his heritage as fast as possible and now lives (I hear) as a prosperous man in smalltown Virginia with his American wife and cute kids.

He was stick thin and quite tiny, with a head that was too large and which looked even more prominent because it was covered in beautiful rich brown curls. His face was built to smile and he wrote poems to me about my inner light and 'transparent soul'. His sister joined our gang and became our intermediary. Every morning as I walked into the school, Skid (for that was his nickname) would be standing, posing against the low wall, his face indiscreetly aglow with love, as I walked past. I knew a letter would be waiting for me in my desk. I would wallow in delicious anticipation until break and rush to the far end of the garden to read it while Lily and Vira kept watch.

There I would read how he had not eaten the night before because he had missed me so much, or how much he loved my eyes. Lovely lies. He wrote out the words of 'Living Doll' by Cliff Richard on a long scroll which he tied with a bow and gave me on my birthday. I began to like myself and became confident enough to express some mild criticism of this boy I adored. We once had a quarrel and he wrote me a Dryden poem, passing it off as his own.

> After the pangs of a desperate love,
> When day and night I have sighed in vain,
> Ah what a pleasure it is to discover,
> In her eyes pity who causes me pain.

I didn't mind. Not at all.

He paid for Vira, Lily and me to go to Elvis and Cliff films with him on a Saturday afternoon. This was so that there would always be some confusion about whose boyfriend he really was. The girls would go in first and he would sneak in when the lights had gone out. We learned to kiss, we held hands tight. I finally understood what all those pop songs were on about. He bought me an expensive ring, which I showed off to everyone during assembly. I said we were 'going steady'. Not many understood what that meant. I was afloat with happiness. Teachers started muttering about my flighty behaviour and my lack of concentration. My skin cleared up, I felt wholly happy, lovely, wanted, envied.

Then Joyce Mann arrived in our lives. An elegant, tall teacher with blonde hair, who wore short tight dresses and walked like a queen. She had style, she had class. We were just about beginning to understand what that meant. She started teaching us literature. After Bhonsle, she was an inspiration. The boys loved her legs. I met Mohammed recently, now a rotund rich businessman in his forties, trying frantically to reclaim his family property back in Uganda. Laughing about Moti and Kololo School, he recalled with passion the effect those legs had on him and his friends. What I never forgot was the utterly cool way she dealt with the kind of catastrophe we girls dreaded more than anything else. One day just as she got up to collect her books to leave, we gasped as we saw a spreading dark red mark across the bottom half of her dress. She knew what it was. She smiled at us, and with superhuman serenity walked away, without even increasing the pace of her walk. What a woman, what poise. By then the word poise meant a lot to us and we spent many a recess trying to walk straight with books on our heads and our toes pointing ever so slightly outwards. When she played Elizabeth Proctor in *The Crucible* at the National, all her devotees, girls and boys went along. (Many did not know the play and thought they were going to see the woman sizzle on stage; they were deeply disappointed to see her dressed up to her chin in dull grey.) She was a wonderful actress and I knew I was right to hate Naseem the way I did.

One of the first texts she decided to do with us was *A Passage to India*, a book I still love more than any other in the world because she made it matter and also because she had the courage to expose us to the deepest effects of the empire on those who ruled and those who were ruled. We all grew up a little after we had finished the book.

She decided to produce *Romeo and Juliet* for the All Africa Drama Competition. We now had a few Africans in our school, so she thought it would be interesting to produce the play using an African family and an Asian family as the Montagues and Capulets, to show, she said, the lack of social contact between the two communities. This was the first time in this school young Africans and Asians had been allowed to grow together, to interact as peers.

I was Juliet. The training with Skid was going to come in handy, because I knew how to be in love: in love secretly, and petrified of being discovered. I am now forty-five and I am still unable to tell my mother about this first bittersweet love affair. John Obwoli, a winsome chap with limpid eyes, played Romeo and Skid got to play Tybalt.

The weeks of rehearsals were intensely thrilling in terms both of the production and the extra time for kissing and cuddling with my young man with the bubbly hair. Puppy love and adolescent ardour leaked all over the place and the air was thick with the scent of unleashed hormones that previously had been bottled up by tight parental control.

Romeo was black and it had not occurred to me to say this at home, swept away as I was by the exhilaration of it all. Papa was as proud as could be because his daughter had learned chunks of Shakespeare.

The performance was at the wonderful theatre at Makerere, one of the first and most prestigious universities that the British had set up in the fifties. None of our families had bothered to come, but the place was packed with kids from all the schools in the area and from other neighbouring countries. I wore sweet-smelling jasmine in my hair and a gold sari. The balcony was festooned with bougainvillaea and roses. The Montagues were dressed in bright shirts and gowns of African printed materials called *kitenge*. We were all bursting with the sense that we were doing something special, something much more important than just putting on a play.

The audience shrieked and gasped when we kissed. Bhonsle let out an audible shout: 'Lord Khrishna, *aree aree*, what is this?' Then we heard some titters and an African voice shouting 'Givu it to ha.' But like true troupers we carried on. Tybalt's anger was too real to be acting and it gave the play an extra edge. The play came second and I won the prize for the best actress. 'Enchanting, beautifully articulate, deeply felt,' said the white adjudicator who wore a peach-coloured knitted outfit and drop pearl earrings. I have always been very good at deeply feeling. She went on to praise the play in general, but added: 'The only problem I had was with Tybalt. Can someone please teach the poor boy to say "v"?' She was referring to the fact that Skid, like many other Asians, said 'dewil, ewil and wery' which was a problem when he had to say 'villain' in every line that he uttered.

Skid's ego was wounded and there was no letter for me on Monday. The cooling off had started. This wasn't simply because of wounded pride. He was getting restless and increasingly impatient with me because I would not go even part of 'all the way' with him and he had found out that there were plenty of girls, even from respectable and rich Asian families, who would. I guess visits to the cinema with three other girls who also insisted on being talked to and a few dozen bruising, but repetitive kisses were unlikely to keep an ambitious 'teenage' boy captive for too long.

More frightening was the reaction at home. This was 1968, when uncertainty among the Asians was mounting. They were appalled, and my 'fame' did not appease them. Outrage had spread across the community. An Asian girl had kissed a black! (I hadn't. There were at least three inches between our lips.) It was more than disgrace: infamy, maybe even a kind of blasphemy or sacrilege, had been committed. I had been defiled. When I wrote a book in 1992 about mixed-race relations in Britain, one Asian father, talking about his feelings when he found out that his daughter had a black boyfriend, said: 'This bastard came to the college. A black boy you know, no class, like an animal. I know about them. I was in Kenya for many years. They were our servants. She ran away with him. I wish she was dead. If she died I would feel this is better for us all. I have not spoken to her since that time, and I will not let her mother speak with her.'

Old terrors rose to the surface. People remembered the grotesque kidnapping of young Arab girls in Zanzibar a few years previously by powerful Africans who had simply helped themselves to the virgins and 'contaminated' them in the eyes of their own families. Three of the girls had eventually killed themselves. For many Africans the kiss was the most porno-graphic thing they had ever seen, because it had broken a terrifying taboo. I was made to feel cheap, dirty and available by many of my black schoolmates. One came up to me, sniggered and said, 'So you like to kiss us, yes? Well we can show you much more, better than your *choroko* boyfriend.' In the subterranean darkness that surrounded our lives lurked age-old sexual hallucinations which could be stimulated even by something as blameless as a school play.

And so much less changes than you imagine. The film *Mississippi Masala*, about the love affair between an Asian girl who had left Uganda as a child and a black American, was heavily censored in Uganda because it was felt that people (especially the Asian returnees much needed by the country as it rebuilds itself) could not cope with such things even in 1992.

Life and art got hopelessly entangled again. By the time the stories reached my family, they were saying things like: 'You know an Asian boy was going to attack that black with a knife to save the honour of your girl, to save respect.' 'These blacks just want our girls. I think it is time to return to India.' Amir slapped me, shook me, banged my head against the rough walls and screamed with anger and pain. My head hurt for days, my heart for far longer. Among all the various things I was not going to be allowed to do any more, the one I could barely cope with was that I was not to go near the stage again. I had been acting since the age of five and my family had always appeared to feel pride and even joy that I appeared to have a talent that, as my mother put it, no gold could buy. It was hard to understand or forgive their ugly turnabout at this, my moment of greatness. What a fate for a best actress who had been convinced by the adjudicator that all she had to do was get on a plane to England and she would end up as the next Julie Christie, my heroine at the time.

My father simply gave up on me and until he died, in November 1970, except for a letter telling me how to stop myself becoming a streetwalker, he did not really speak to me again. That did not stop him breaking into my small locked green suitcase and tearing up all my letters from Skid and my precious photographs with him taken by chubby-cheeked Hasmukh, another friend who helped to service this love which was clearly not made in heaven, and needed all our wits just to keep going.

The school barely knew how to react. On the one hand there was all that kudos because the production had received acclaim – and from white people. My, my. Patel could hardly throw a fit at somebody as naturally imperious as Joyce Mann. So with a smile even more false than usual he pretended that he was delighted with all of us. Our success was not mentioned during assembly, but some girl who had received a certificate of merit from Chottabhai for her first successful dance routine was applauded, and given a Parker pen. Patel did not, could not look at me, though. His fury was all the more effective because it was caged in and you knew from the way his gnarled hands were clenched and the squint in his eyes that he was ready to kill. Parents had been in to complain. One or two even demanded that black male students should be separated from the Asian girls. Some rich families, who donated the odd sum to the school, were the most vociferous in such demands. Patel knew that such an action would be political suicide, so he let

132

things be. He managed to convince my mother that even I would be redeemed under his regime.

The crisis blew over in time, although the story survives in the far corners of the world. John and I remained close friends. He was mad about Indian music, Indian history and knew more about both than I did. The last I heard from him, he had gone out to India to work as part of the diplomatic mission. I had a letter from him when he was in quarantine because he had failed to get the shots he needed. He wrote: 'I am looking out and I can see beautiful Indian women in their flowing clothes, the men on their old bicycles, the whole world. Dying to get myself out there.' Six months later he was killed in a car crash outside New Delhi. Painful ironies.

And it got worse. I did so well in my exams that year that Patel decided to make me head prefect. His words to me were as terrifying as ever: 'Yes, Yasmin, you know all the tricks, there is a bit of *saitan* in you. So you should be my head girl. You have your eyes open and I will have my eyes on you all the time. Together we will improve the school and straighten you out.'

13

At home, my mother found it harder and harder to protect me from the vindictive behaviour of my brother and his wife, my Zarbhabhi. Their wedding was full of triumphalism on one side and mortification on the other. The photographs have recorded it all for posterity. There is one where Amir is pulling my hair. It is meant to be a joke. I look, and was, almost anorexic and tortured. Lily and Vira are watching pitifully and helplessly. I did get a beautiful dress, though, and that sort of compensated for things. The pleasure did not last. By the third party, my friends were teasing hurtfully that I always wore the same old dress and I had to beg to wear some of theirs to the next one.

And as life at home degenerated further, my mother's health began to deteriorate too. She had always been sickly, but she had been able to rise above her ailments by searching for some new cure and incessantly talking about the miraculous effects of vinegar or bicarbonate of soda or both: 'Try to rub the gums with this they will stop the bleeding and they will be so white.' Now all her potency, her vigour, evaporated. Her son was almost indifferent to her, his wife completely in control. My mother was given money for the housekeeping, and like a servant expected to account for every penny. They would accuse her of hiding money and she would weep. They were right, of course. Having been exposed all her life had taught my mother to extract savings out of thin air.

She now lives on thirty-five pounds a week supplementary pension and is constantly offering to lend us the four hundred pounds she has saved up. All her hopes that her son would somehow compensate for the lack of male support in her life were shattered and she did not know how to deal with it except to become obscenely humble, to try to please him and win some crumb of approval or recognition. He, on the other hand, having finally liberated himself was, for a long while, indifferent to all her affection and expectations. Family pathologies do not die. They reincarnate and come back as more vicious versions of themselves.

Friends who visited the new and posh house in Kololo which we moved to after my brother got married, said how pleased they were that my mother no longer had to work so hard and that thanks to her son she at last had a house with a garden and some respite. My mother nodded brightly and agreed, and said that she had God to thank for her good fortune.

Once when visitors had left, I found my mother on the floor, having a fit, gurgling, her eyes rolling, her body rigid, looking as if it would rupture. I sat on her and tried to hold her tightly clenched hands. My father emerged from the bedroom, in his pyjamas, still holding his precious book – this was what he now did all day long – and stood there, looking stunned but useless, screaming for someone to get a doctor. My brother and his wife were out and it was a neighbour who finally came and took control. As soon as she entered the house my father went back to his reading. For years afterwards this would happen to my mother from time to time. I learned what to do – put a spoon over her tongue, sit on her legs and get the servant to hold her arms, try and get a tablet into her while she was thrashing around as if she could bear the humiliations of her life no more. Then I would sit by her for all those long hours when she was absolutely still, her spirit dissipated, afraid that she would never wake up again and knowing that if she didn't I would lose the only person in the whole world who truly cared about me.

When Farah, Zarbhabhi and Amir's daughter, was born, a small shaft of light came into all our lives and although she cried night and day (perhaps she already knew) with her came a little faith that the fissures between all of us might heal. Teresa her ayah, a big woman with a sullen face and a finely tuned sense of self-respect, was the only one who refused to spoil Farah and with her my niece was like any ordinary happy child. With my mother, who loved her insanely, Farah was incessantly demanding, needing to fill some kind of bottomless pit of insecurity. As time went on, we became competitive, all vying for Farah's attention and blaming each other when she behaved monstrously. In New York now, a woman of extraordinary beauty and imagination, Farah can still evoke in all of us a special, exciting, addictive kind of affection. Her love for my son is as consuming as mine was for her. Sometimes good too drips down the generations.

But this was also the time when my brother seemed to begin his descent into self-pity, perhaps because that made it easier to cope with his own complicated emotions – his love for my mother and his need to tear himself away, his devotion for his wife which made him appear a wimp (and this he was not), his deep sense that he was failing everybody – he transformed himself into the victim preyed upon. What began as an excuse, ended up as a strong conviction. He developed a slight hunch, a melancholic expression, and broodiness soon after this, looking deep and long into his beer glass and spending at least two hours every day (three at weekends) in his bathtub where he could be away from the emotional lynch mob in his life. There were so many fights in our home at this time that it felt strangely empty on those rare days when words, fists and things were not flying about.

My English husband, with soft blue eyes and a voice like a warm gentle breeze, brought up in a household where it was better to choke to death than spit out your anger, finds it impossibly difficult when I erupt in our house. I try to convince him that these outbursts show that I am a child of nature, spontaneous and alive. In fact they come from a compulsion to kill something before it grows big enough to hurt me. It would be wonderful if he could hurl a coffee cup in a fit of anger just sometimes, so I wouldn't feel that I was guilty of the lack of self-control which helped our conquerors believe that they were saving us from ourselves.

Skid's passion for me was fading fast. The end came in two parts. We had started going out with a rather fancy crowd, and Skid was becoming a bit of a snob and aspiring to greater status. He was enraged one day when he discovered that I had neglected to shave my armpits and was wearing a sleeveless dress when we were out with one of his rich friends. He was also angry that I had not brushed the talcum powder out of my hair – a trick I used to get rid of the grease without washing it. He and I knew then that I would never be the kind of society belle he thought he was going to need.

Two days later, he had further proof that I was not the girl for him. He got a key to a flat belonging to a friend and took me there, clearly with serious intentions. I had enough good sense to realise that it would not be wise to allow myself to be deflowered, especially by a pretentious twerp with few prospects and still unable to say 'v'. There were other powerful deterrents. Most of us still believed that you could get pregnant even by using the same towel as a man. And there was no way anybody could buy condoms because Mr Patel, the pharmacist, who knew everybody in the community, made it his business to keep a strict and observant eye on who was buying the balloons, as he called them. And besides, I had cherished dreams of a wedding night with a huge bed full of flowers and a moon peeping into my face from the window. But more than anything else, the reason for not taking any risks was fear of my family and for that I remain grateful to this day.

I sat in my white shirt and grey skirt, arms clutched across my front and refused to comply. I was quite proud that all he had ever got to do was hold my hands and kiss me until my lips hurt. He cajoled, he flattered, he gave me a present. Imported chocolates. How cheap can you get? Or rather, how cheap do you think you can get it for?

Then he threatened to leave me. I was stunned because I was still besotted with the idea of being in love and aware enough to know that somebody like me was not likely to get another boyfriend too quickly. I cried, I begged, I swore I would die, but I did not let him touch me below the neck.

Well he did go on to get someone more smooth and sophisticated, a girl who had 'poise', expensive taste and, I trust, more of a sense of adventure than I had shown. In the months afterwards, my life was doused with sorrow. At school I worked till I was ready to drop and wandered around careful never to smile, looking lost, forlorn. At home, with all the other emotional disarray around, all I felt able to do was get into my mother's long dress and listen to sad Jim Reeves and Cliff Richard records borrowed from my friends. I thought I would never climb out of my deep despair. But I did, not only then but again and again, each time imagining that I was buried for ever in grief.

Miss Mary felt so worried about me that she took me off to a 'friend' who turned out to be a Catholic priest heavily into converting the natives. For hours he droned on in a voice tediously pious and self-satisfied. Was I tired of life? Yes, very. Had I ever thought of suicide? Yes, and even tried it once – a friend had told me to try four aspirins with Coca-Cola. Nothing had happened except I burped a lot for a few hours. Did I believe in God? Yes sort of, though I wasn't sure which one. Was I suffering because I was being pushed into an arranged marriage? No, silly. Did I realise that the God I worshipped was a matter that only I could decide? Did I know about the love of God, and the Son of God, Christ? I told him the story about the monitor lizard in the bible shop. He didn't seem amused and I was bored so we parted, and on the way back Miss Mary kept on babbling about the sin of suicide.

When my birthday came round that year, Miss Mary baked me a cake in school and gave me a book. It was *The Kenya Settler's Cookery Book and Household Guide* first published by the St Andrew's Church, Nairobi in 1958. It had recipes for baked eggs in gravy, devils on horseback and treacle pudding. The only thing I ever made from it was scrambled eggs with tomatoes. There were some curry recipes including one which said: 'curry (a good Indian)' which had as its main ingredients peach jam, milk, gravy or soup; browsing through the book one day many years later in my flat in Oxford, I discovered a list of useful 'Orders to Servants' in Swahili. They include 'Leave off talking', 'Enough of words', 'You are free from 2 o'clock to 4 o'clock, but at any other time, you must be on duty', 'Go and wash yourself', 'Do not be sulky' and 'You are insolent. You must look pleasant (or pleased).' Many other essentials of life feature. How to give people with 'low appetite' albumen soup and the 'Management of Sitting Hen' which teaches you how to get a broody hen to do her duty.

She was nice, Miss Mary, after all and in her own clumsy way felt for us. But she was friendless. People like her were to be pitied, or so the people said. Through no fault of their own, they found themselves a bit of this and a bit of that. Milkshakes is how Mr Bhonsle would refer to the Anglo–Indians: 'sorrowfully lost the ancient traditions of Mother India and also the great English civilisation, you can't taste the milk and you can't enjoy the strawberries, just a mess.' It was certainly true that Miss Mary seemed to be less weighty, less consequential than most other people but that was no excuse to treat her the way Jim Barrow did, leaving her for Florry, the floozy who wore snake-shaped bangles on her upper arm and who licked his ears openly in his sports car.

All this agony and craving meant I was seethingly ready for my next love affair. Like a ripe and ready to explode piece of fruit, exuding a powerful over-pungent scent, I awaited the bite. It came upon me unexpectedly in the back of a car. My friend Nazira, who was tall, ravishing and knew how to apply eyeliner in a straight line, and who had taught me how to iron my hair so it looked like Jean Shrimpton's, had a date. He was smaller than her, had a goatee beard, and a car which made him much more attractive to all three of us than even he thought he deserved. His friend, Sky, was beautiful. That was all, because that was all he needed to be. And he was bold, because within minutes of sitting in the back seat with him, he was toying with my hand and I was panting for more.

I was more than slightly flattered that he was my partner at a party where I knew Skid was going to be with his flash new girlfriend, although for the entire evening Sky's eyes were roaming around gazing at what he was missing out on. I should have learned something about him then. I didn't, and twenty years later I was to live to regret my folly.

By this time, I had become a seasoned liar at home, as one does at this age. Claiming I was staying at Nazira's house for the evening, I would end up with a face made up like Elizabeth Taylor in *Cleopatra* and fancy clothes that were too big for me, although I made sure that my breasts were suitably prominent by stuffing cotton wool into my bra.

I became a stunningly good dancer and could do the twist, the cha–cha–cha and the bossa nova (at least that is what we thought it was) better than all the girls. I think it was because although I loved my virginity – it proved that I was in control – I was willing to abandon all restraint on the dance floor and display a wildness when most of my friends were more cautious. And I loved boys slinking up to me and saying things like: '*Yaar*, you are the bombshell baby of Bombay' (a popular Hindi song at the time which featured a fleshy nightclub dancer who could move like a rattlesnake) although by now I preferred to think of myself as the heroine in *West Side Story*.

This is not retrospective embellishment. In a completely tangible way, all our cultural and moral messages were either reinforced or toppled by what we were seeing in the cinema. Floating around so far removed from any actual historical connections, we chose who we were from one of those all-embracing continental menus. So the battles that were emerging between the generations were not simply tradition versus modernity, but between which films gave us the best lessons on life and how we should conduct ourselves. Our own elders were too fond of declaring their own distance from those folk in India and Pakistan who were so 'backward'. 'No sanitation in those places, you know, have to take your own Dettol [pronounced Ditol] and wash everything in it. Also the servants' hands,' people like Nusratbai would say after she returned from one of her trips to Bombay where she went to have gold jewellery sets made for her numerous and unattractive daughters who would need all the help they could get in order to attract husbands. One still ended up a very bitter spinster who wears dresses which defiantly reveal a dark, hairy and large cleavage.

Getting to these parties and back was always difficult as I had to crouch down in case anybody who knew my family saw me. I was always worried sick but delirious too with the sense of danger I carried with me. For I was genuinely afraid of provoking my brother's volatile temper which had got significantly worse since he started feeding it self-pity. These days a wonderful calm has settled on his face – he seems to have found his old self, I realise how much of what he had become was a response to having to always be responsible to others and never just to himself.

Nazira's parents were open, kind, uncomplicated and warm. There were no dark and broody corners or lurking terrors anywhere in their modest little house. Moss and Poss, as they were universally known, took me into their lives and never asked for anything back. They laughed, talked to each other about inconsequential things; their lives seemed so normal. They weren't even aware of their generosity to me or the overwhelming solace I found in their home and their kind of love. On my birthdays, when I needed money for my school fees at a time when things at home were unspeakable, when I did well in my exams, Moss and Poss would step in imperceptibly and make sure I knew they were there for me. My mother too found deep comfort with these remarkable people.

In 1972, when expelled by Idi Amin, Moss and Poss found themselves in a small town in South Carolina with a handful of other Ugandan refugees who had nowhere else to go. Just when they were ready to retire and settle down to a contented life of mosque, gossip, evenings spent on balconies taking the air and listening to old Hindi songs, they found themselves living in smalltown, small-minded America. Here, they faced suspicion and exploitation – burning their arms as they carried enormous trays of hot bread in a bakery, their family split up and never knowing what lay ahead. But talk to them about this time and they will only say how grateful they feel to be alive and to have had work and shelter.

Their modesty and goodness is so profound, I know they would not want me to tell the world about what they did for me. It isn't just the fact that they treated me like their own daughter, but that they made me laugh and understand how love in a family can sustain people. The way they would call me Joan of Arc when I had that terrible haircut or the ease with which they could tell me off. The last few years have taken their toll, but Moss and Poss never see it like that. Their religious faith just enhances their lives and those of others. The last time we met in Uganda, Moss gave me one of her beautiful old gold bangles. One day Leila, my daughter, will have it. She will not believe the stories I will tell her about them, because she is growing up in a country where such things are rare, even amongst our own people.

My love for Sky was sealed the day I saw him play his drum kit at his school dance. In the brand new hall, with impossible echoes and far too much chattering, I watched this Adonis with his aquiline nose and mediocre talent. The song was 'Black is Black'. His love for me was properly established the day I passed my A levels with resounding success and became the sort of student all parents and teachers pointed to as an example. I don't think it was an entirely cynical move. Anyway it fitted in with his cool image to have an unconventional girlfriend. I was wearing a lilac dress with a sailor collar, a present from my brother who had been to England on a business trip and had come back with wonderful things for all of us. We were by now managing to have some periods of relative sanity and even pleasure in our family. Farah was growing up into a delightful little toddler and some of the bitterness was dissolving.

Standing under the stars, Sky kissed me and said: 'I guess you know by now that I love you.' I was over the moon, relishing the cool way he delivered himself into my heart and the promise contained in those few words. I burnt all other boats on the horizon including Abdul (my other suitor who was ready to be engaged to me before I went to university and had bought a beautiful necklace to make him less resistible). That love, which began on 9 August 1968, in spite of the occasional foray into profligacy and faithlessness, served us till 20 January 1988 when Sky departed ten days before our son's tenth birthday to spend the rest of his life in the arms of another, younger woman.

I last spoke to him in 1989. He looked absurd on that day wearing some extraordinary American clothes with meaningless slogans all over them. I was pathetic, still weeping for him, and begging him to come back and keep our family, our love going. He wanted us to be friends. I couldn't oblige and I am sorry. I don't believe friends are failed lovers.

14

But although this remarkably raw pain I still feel makes it difficult to reflect properly on this part of the story and I feel impelled to push on, to get it over and done with, there is so much more to say about that love which may indeed have started as a cheap imitation of what we thought we longed for when we listened to pop songs and watched romantic British and American films, but it was also a whole lot more. In some ways it was the thrill of a generation discovering an entire range of emotions for the first time. Before the sixties, affection based on the interdependence of partners was something that grew slowly and steadily, building up right through to the twilight years. You never saw any body contact between the sexes, and discretion was such a well developed social tool that you never knew whether most relationships were happy or tormented, except perhaps by a slightly haunted look in the eyes of the people who prayed most fervently in the mosque. Suddenly people in my generation knew what it felt like to anticipate the sight and touch of the one you loved, to feel the rush of pleasure in your body and mind, to experience that heightened sense that you were living and feeling at a pitch that your parents could not even imagine. In fact they did not even have the vocabulary to describe what we were feeling. Or doing.

Sky and I felt that love, and both our mothers, each deeply disappointed though accepting of what fate had given them, rejoiced in what we had found. For twenty years, that passionate love sustained us both through the pain of exile, of self-doubt, of transformations that we could never have envisaged in the dreamy lives we had led until we left Uganda. And though there is much to regret about what happened later, what we felt was unsullied and immeasurable and what it meant was much more perhaps than it could bear.

In other ways too, at this time, it felt as if the world was indeed ours the way it had never been before, although Asians were still always strung up to be pecked at by politicians every time they needed an excuse for the monumental economic and political failures of the government. President Milton Obote was devious and paranoid as a leader, capable of producing terrible chaos and violence but somehow remaining unadulterated himself. An old woman who cleaned our rooms at Makerere University, explaining why Amin was better than Obote, once said to me in Swahili: 'Don't ever trust a man who is too clean after he has eaten or killed.' In the end he managed to conceal the blood on others too. In the horrific years that followed our expulsion in 1972, the years when scores of black Ugandans had nowhere to go but to their deaths, it is clear that the numbers of people tortured and massacred on the orders of Obote before he was toppled and after he came back from exile in the eighties was far greater than those who died under Idi Amin. But he did not appear rough and obviously menacing like Amin did, so the world simply ignored what he was doing.

In 1969, prominent students throughout the country had been invited by Obote to spend a month at the State House in order to understand what the government was trying to do. This canny strategy was put forward by the president himself because he was very worried about the student upheavals in Europe and the United States. It was a frightening time, because we were constantly being tempted to open up and discuss issues freely but we knew (though at times it was made easy for us to forget), as one does when one has lived in newly emerging nations, that you do so at your peril. Three delegates, all Bagandans, did in fact mysteriously disappear after some heated debates.

Obote himself came from a small northern cattle-owning tribe and he particularly hated the Bagandans, the biggest and most educated tribe in Uganda. These were the people who almost naturally conducted themselves as if they were born to rule. They were the first to have converted to Christianity and to welcome early white explorers. The British paid them back for their co-operation by always supporting their king, the Kabaka, and building them special schools, like Budo, schools where they got a good, solid, British Public education and from where, it was expected black Etonians would emerge to take up their rightful place. And in some ways the whole of the post-independence history of Uganda has been the culling of this group to keep them down and out. But some things outlast even massacres. You can always tell a Budo boy. He is immaculate in his speech and manners, just ever so slightly superior, which you soon cease to mind because he is so very clever and smooth. And although they were and are the greatest lawyers and academics in the country, they never did take up their place at the helm. Instead hundreds of thousands lost their lives because the rulers feared and loathed them simply for having had that destiny thrust upon them. As one Bagandan who still lives in exile, still fears even to talk to people like me said: 'They all hate us because they know that we are better educated, better able than they are. But they also know that our parents were so busy telling us to read books that they forgot to teach us how in our country we needed to learn about guns not books. I feel God has given up on Africa and although I hate living here in this shitty UK I will never go back.' This man is an economist. He is working as a decorator.

There were only three Asians among the fifty or so students. Obote would play games with us at dinner time. 'So, *wahindi*, how much money left for England this week, eh? Eh, you Patels are all the same. But you know I like you people, I wish we could learn your dirty tricks. But you are welcome here, just no tricks, please.' He never laughed although, sensing our discomfort, he would claim it was a joke. At least I could honestly tell him that at that time my father did not even have a bank account. I did feel a certain pride about this fact. All three of us were desperately disappointed to be judged by the sins of our fathers when we wanted so much to show that we were different. But as South Africa will undoubtedly one day reveal to us, you cannot put past iniquities to bed quite so easily even for higher principles. The need for retribution always arises.

Obote was indeed terrifyingly ordered and tidy, especially when we were eating in the vast and beautiful state banqueting room with cutlery and crockery all inscribed as still Her Majesty's. Young women in black dresses and white aprons carrying soup tureens would visibly shake when they approached him because he hated a drop of anything going astray. His long-suffering wife, who was a Bagandan herself (many believed this was a marriage of political convenience at a time when Obote thought it was important to court the tribe instead of crushing it) sat imperiously through these events, her loftiness barely covering up her fear of this cruel man with a strange conical hairstyle and huge gaps between his teeth. Like prison bars, one delegate said they were.

I met Idi Amin at this time too, when he was the head of the Ugandan army. We were presented with the not very welcome chance to ask him anything we wanted to know about the army. Folly rather than doughtiness prompted me to ask this vast man, who could have stamped me to death and not even noticed, why there were no Asians in the Ugandan army. He roared with wicked laughter and said that it was because they did not know how to make *choroko* (dhal) in the army and because Asians were such weaklings. The next time I saw him was in 1971 when he had crowned himself not only president, but head of everything including the university. He arrived in his chancellor's regalia and insisted on individually handing over degree certificates to over five hundred graduates. The day was long and hot, but that was not the only reason we were all dripping sweat and ruining our posh new clothes. The humiliation and fear of bowing down before an unpredictable brute made this event more memorable than most graduations. As I watched Sky go up and get his degree, I felt a hysterical impulse to laugh and also a fear that should Amin turn, whoever was nearest would be his victim. He knew he was despised by the learned, and after courting their respect in this rather pathetic way he turned against them with a ferocity that devastated the intelligentsia for at least a decade.

But towards the end of the sixties, in spite of these dark hints of what was to come, there was a palpable sense of hope, unity and progress especially among the emerging younger generations and most especially at Makerere University. And even a campus demonstration which brought in the troops, firing at random (none dead, several injured, many people never seen again) did not allay our dangerous optimism. The three years I spent there were among the happiest in my life. I was finally away from the constant grief and acrimony of our family life and although I missed my mother hugely and felt that I had abandoned her in the midst of a thorny thicket which would continue to tear at her and might even kill her, I was unable and unwilling to share her pain or to surrender my own young life to it.

She was exalted that I was not only going to university – the first and only one in our entire family to do so even over the next twenty years – but that I had achieved the best A-level results in the country despite all the obstacles placed in my way by my brother and his wife. The nagging was relentless: I was using too much electricity when I studied into the night; I wasn't helping enough with my niece Farah and nephew Salim, both children I loved to death and, in spite of my tender age, as if they were my own; I had too many distractions, too many 'bad' friends and, worst of all, I didn't care for my mother or I would try and be more pliant and obedient. At times, very rarely, my mother, worn out emotionally, would add her voice to this litany, mainly because she craved peace, and peaceful sleep most of all. All her life she has taken sleeping tablets; she says she cannot sleep otherwise because the past and the present so crowd out her tired brain. I can sleep anywhere, any time. It is so often our mothers who take up our pain and troubles, so we can find repose.

But for a while, a smidgen of fondness had emerged in my brother after I passed my A levels and it did cost him. Literally. He said he would pay for me to learn driving – 'as many lessons as you need' – and buy me a car so I could stay at home and attend college. Not wishing to cross him, and in order to exploit this generosity, I did not inform him that nothing, not even promises of my own room, table lamp and all the electricity in the world, nor any threats, would persuade me to stay in that house after June of that year.

So I started driving lessons with a recommended motoring school and a driving instructor called Milton who always dressed in perfectly ironed safari suits. Now, back home, included in the initial payments was the standard bribe for the test centre. Milton was a brilliant teacher though he always smelt of stale *waragi* and boiled chicken. But I was a lousy learner and after thirty-eight lessons, which left us both worn out with effort, I failed my test in spite of the bribe. It was because I told them I had never seen any of the road signs they showed me on a chart. This imposing man said to me: 'Maybe, madam, you should learn these before I test you. In Uganda we are very serious about these sorts of things. Take her away, sir.'

I think this failure was very important to their sense of self-respect, their need to know that they too had standards and were not completely for sale. I really cannot blame my poor brother for being furious with me on this occasion and I suppose it served me right that for years whenever he wanted me to see how unappreciative I was, this was brought up. I must pay the poor man back for this at least when I am rich. I think my mother too was saddened that the plan came to nothing. I only learned to drive in my forties when I had to fend for myself and my son on my own.

Looking back, leaving was a grotesquely selfish thing to do to my mother. I can see, absolutely vividly, the pain in her eyes when I left, but also the courage with which she supported my escape and her sheer joy that because I had got a scholarship, she would not need to ask my brother for money for me. A little less begging, a little more dignity regained for a woman who is more proud than anything else. Proud and without rancour, even now when there is so little time left and her life is still not without struggle.

I have had an easier life, but at the age of forty-five, I am full of angry lava which rumbles barely beneath the surface and erupts frequently enough to make Colin, my husband, lover and friend, worry about my long-term well-being and I suspect his own sanity. Where does this anger come from? he asks me burrowing beyond my eyes to see the source of the red-hot liquid. How do I answer that? I know some of it has deep historical roots in times when life seemed so tough and it should have been carefree, when people who should have felt proud of me were mean and nasty, and then it was the bitter aftertaste when I had liberated myself and betrayed my mother by leaving her behind to fend for herself embattled, watching my brother grow away from her and my father growing into himself. This internal fury of mine was then damagingly topped up by the rage I felt when my ex-husband left, for no really good reason, it seemed to me, other than the fact that the other woman was younger, had a smaller waistline, and probably satisfied his need for self-delusion and a rush back to the future when his receding hair and aching, breaking back were signalling the onset of middle age.

What is more alarming is that our son, Ari, now seventeen, is just as angry and volatile as me. In his case because his childhood was so secure, blameless, nurturing. Both his parents wanted so desperately not to repeat the pain in his life that they had lived through and to give him the security he would need with parents who had no country or base to call their own. Then, suddenly, that safety was gone, eternity was only ten years long. And although I have done my best, like my mother did her best, and Colin has been there to clear the debris and make something else, something different grow, I know that one day, a long time from now, the person who loves my son will want to know where his terrible wrath comes from. I hope he will be fortunate enough to find somebody like I have, someone who will be able to isolate the moment of madness from the long unyielding sense of an unjust past which began the day his father left and his mother was too wounded to cope with the situation, to protect her son as she should have done. At least for the first few months.

The day I was leaving for university came. Only my mother and the little ones said goodbye. Farah, I knew I would miss terribly, because although she was a demanding little brat, she understood the nature of tempestuous love even as a toddler. I have a daughter now, an independent, reckless lass, Leila, who reminds me of Farah when I left home. The same round chubby face and Singaporean eyes, and something already formed which comes across as defiance or maybe self-defini-tion. Farah is now a sassy New Yorker, with an art gallery, and a nose for what is likely to be trendy. One day, I hope she can find the love she is seeking, someone who sees how vulnerable she is and can protect her from herself and her own cynicism, the result of seeing so much pain in the relationships around her when she was only a child.

By this time my father had more or less disappeared under the bedclothes except when he came out to eat and to see to the other basic necessities of life. He looked even more gaunt than before, his cheeks, deep dark hollows, his eyes moist and grey like his hair. I was callous: I didn't care about the terror he was feeling and the end of hope in his life. I wish he was alive, so I could talk to him. I knew he hated me going because by this time his belief in education for his daughter had drowned in a kind of mad fear for her virginity. He did not speak to me about any of this. Towards me he kept up a venomous silence, but I knew whenever my mother ventured anywhere near him just before and for a long time after I left he would send forth a torrent of verbal abuse about *her* daughter.

He was right of course to worry about my virginity – it didn't survive eight weeks into the college term, and that was what really delighted me at the prospect of leaving home. But that did not stop me feeling cruelly misunderstood and ill-treated by my own father.

My mother made me some parathas and *achaar* to take to college. She had also bought some Sanatogen liquid tonic because she was convinced that I would die of starvation in the hall of residence respectfully still (and even now) called Mary Stuart Hall, or the Box because it was a ghastly, tall sixties tower block, an awful blot on the wonderful landscape.

By this time Sky had been at university for a year. He had sold his precious drum kit after I started yet another row after yet another Saturday evening spent sitting around being a reluctant groupie. With the money, he bought a handsome silver and orange Honda 125 motorbike. What with his looks, bum-clasping jeans and now this, I knew the competition for him would get even more intense and I had to watch him. That anxiety was with me for years, and I only began to lose it when I was in my thirties and subtle changes took place in the way I saw myself. I began to think of myself as just as attractive and desirable. He left soon after that. My confidence in myself stayed.

In the beginning, though, it was my own mind making mischief. For a good long while, he never really let even his eyes stray too far beyond the superficial admiring look. And when I sat on his bike, my spots and greasy hair gone at last, in high heels, flagrantly short miniskirts and yellow satin hot pants, I did feel luckier than Jean Shrimpton and now when I look at the fading, curled-up photos of that time, I can see how happiness can make you look prettier than you were ever meant to.

I had been with Sky for nearly three years before we had sex. His patience was not particularly extraordinary because he feared the consequences of being found out as much as I did. Besides, this was a way of showing me respect, of letting me know that I mattered a great deal. The only time his hormones could not cope was a clandestine trip we made in a good old-fashioned Victorian train to the coast with slow rhythmic movements which invited you to make love. There we were in an oak-panelled cabin, with lovely dim lights and brass fittings. There for two nights, together and alone, and he still had to make do with a little above-the-waist snogging, and exaggerated declarations of love.

But almost as soon as I had arrived at university and hung up my clothes in the sparse room I was sharing with two African girls, Sophie and Jane, I knew that the impossible was rapidly becoming the inevitable and that it was only a matter of (very little) time. What made it all so much easier and more natural was the fact that my two room-mates were so much more open about their sexuality than as Asian girls we had ever been allowed to be. In fact even as I write this, I am scared that my mother will finally find out what I was up to at university and it might still make her angry or (worse) make her cry.

My son, trying to trip me up and throw me off the puritanical attitudes I now display – it is the only way for the folk of the sixties to bring up sane children – asked me how much drugs and sex I 'did' in those flamboyant times. No drugs, I tell him, and sex at twenty only with your father, and that was pretty daring.

15

But when I started university in 1970, so many years after independence, it was rare for Asian and African girls to share rooms. It was also rare, I later discovered, for different Ugandan tribes to share their space. But what you saw when you went into the dining room was the visual segregation that offended the eye, although here were practical reasons for this. Two tables were for vegetarians, which many of the Asian girls were. The usual bad food was served up: fried eggs which you could stand up on their side, they were so stiff, beans, beans and more beans plus sometimes some stringy meat and *matoke*, green bananas which would bloat you up for hours. The first thing I wanted to do when I went back after twenty-two years was to feel that weight in my stomach again.

Makerere University had a delightful campus, high on a hill full of bougainvillaea, hibiscus flowers and Nandi flame trees. The branches of these trees spread out to create huge shady spaces and when you lay under them in mid-afternoon, looking at the red-orange blooms and hundreds of dark seed pods hanging down like fat worms, it was hard not to feel that heaven was indeed a perfect moment on earth. We had everything and more. The main building was white, huge and imposing, with a bell tower, panelled walls and an impressive staircase which a tired old man spent his life cleaning and polishing. Sometimes I watched him taking a tiny pin, wrapping a film of cotton wool around it, dipping this in some dark polish and carefully trying to deal with a brash scratch made with a key by some uppity student. In 1994, when I went back to the main hall to revisit the stage where we had performed *Romeo and Juliet* and where we had later danced till the sun came up, the smell of urine in this building was so overwhelming I threw up in the car park.

During the same visit I met a Makerere student selling vegetables in the central market. That was the only way he could carry on with his studies. He asked me incredulously if it was true that in our day, we had porridge and sausages for breakfast.

Yes, but more importantly, I told him, in 1970 Makerere was a distinguished and possibly utopian place, where students and lecturers felt incredibly privileged and powerful. We were going to make the future and break from the past which had kept so many down and out, and some of us were going to make amends. We were writing a new history which showed the world that Africa was neither intellectually barren nor uncivilised before the European, greedy for wealth and status, conferred that dishonest past on an entire continent. We were making a new destiny for ourselves – black, brown and white Ugandans together for the first time and able to think in a way our parents simply could not have.

The English department was introducing a completely new syllabus, which included not only Shakespeare and Chaucer, but new voices which had never heard or seen the sound and light of day. I had two black lecturers who did not like me at all because they were committed to wholesale Africanisation. I wanted at times to kill them, but I was nevertheless astounded by the force of their creative power. Piu Zirimu was one of them, a thin, intense man with a beard, glasses and haughty air who ignored my contributions during tutorials to focus on some young black man whom I (always) thought was much less interesting than me. He was often dismissive of the few other Asians on the course (my people study chemistry, law and medicine, not 'wasting time silly stories') and you could sense that people like him were already becoming possessive about who had the right to appraise the writing of 'true' Africans. How futile is this quest for authenticity in an eclectic world. When I heard that both he and his wife had died within months of each other, I felt the loss deeply. Another teacher wrote astonishing raw poetry with not a daffodil or dell in sight. He wrote instead about the voluptuous pleasures to be had with an ageing prostitute and we felt the delights of subversion even then. We had to learn to value work which at first did not feel as grand as what we believed real literature ought to be: writing as bare and heroically defiant as in the short story, 'Mrs Plum', by the black South African writer Ezekiel Mphahlele:

> My madam's name was Mrs Plum. She loved dogs and Africans and said that everyone must follow the law even if it hurt. These were three big things in madam's life . . . Madam is a tall woman. Not slender, not fat. She moves slowly and speaks slowly. Her face looks very wise, her forehead seems to tell me she has a strong liver: she is not afraid of anything. Her eyes are always swollen, the lower eyelids like a white person who has not slept for many nights or like a large frog.

No one in the West has ever really bothered to pick up some of this truly felt work by the post-independence writers of Africa, and the gross ignorance of British academics when it comes to Africa even in the 1990s is hard to forgive. Can you imagine the sense of discovery we must have felt when, one after another, such writers began to be incorporated into our understanding of what makes great art and the insights that such writing can give our lives? The difference is important enough to labour the point. When I was able to enter and fathom the writing of, say, Jane Austen, the feeling was one of victory, of barriers crossed, of breakthrough into a literature we were expected never truly to understand, but which you had to learn if you wanted to be a somebody. When I read new African and Caribbean writers, the joy came out of finding an echo, a meaning for our lives which until then had seemed so irrelevant to the grand cultural projects of the world and people who had the power to make things matter.

Compared with the narrow-minded, protectionist British academics I later met when I came to England, the white tutors at Makerere were extraordinarily receptive. Even those who believed that independence was an unnecessary interruption in a country which had been chugging along nicely, and who therefore looked cantankerous a lot of the time, even these individuals were ardently in love with all things African. Things, mind you, not often the people (except those black women some of the hard-drinking, middle-aged men picked up at nightclubs who gave them such a good time that they would buy them new dresses and sometimes walk about holding their hands, stiffly and in spite of themselves), not least because they had such extraordinarily good lives. On the campus at Makerere, the lecturers lived in gorgeous bungalows with lovely gardens and the ubiquitous veranda on which they would sip their perfectly mixed cocktail, served by servants who revered them because they were *mwalimus*, teachers, and praying, I imagine, for their good fortune to continue. Some were people of mediocre talent who knew they were reaping more reward than they deserved, and we certainly had one such lecturer in our department whose way out of this painful self-knowledge was to be petulant all the time. I wonder how these people then learned to cope when they had to leave their beloved Uganda and make do within the ugly walls of badly lit British polytechnics and colleges where you are only slightly more respected than an inner city social worker.

And how did the others survive the descent into such an existential hell? Those genuine enthusiasts and compelling teachers at Makerere who had avoided old world exhaustion and cynicism and were conscious of their responsibilities in building up a future for the newly emerging country. Those who were infected by a love of East Africa which, like malaria, never ever really leaves you.

They knew they mattered, we mattered and what we were going to do with our lives mattered most of all. People like Mrs McPherson in the English department, a vigorous lady who inspired us as a teacher, but put us in our place and instilled an eternal modesty which in the end served to help keep us on our toes. Her love for Makerere was absolute and for years afterwards, and even now, she painstakingly produces newsletters which keep hundreds of us in touch. In those grim days between 1972 and 1986, when so much blood was being shed in that country, the typed, always supremely diplomatic, McPherson newsletter would inform us how many old members had 'sadly died' – become victims of the killing orgies – and how many were now in Denver, Nairobi or Harare, doing very well, getting married, alive. I still fear and respect this grand old lady who helped me immeasurably to believe I could get into Oxford, who wrote wonderful accounts of my talents to a prince, interested in education, and persuaded him to pay for me to go there.

Then there was Jonathan Kingdon in the Art department. A huge, bearded, fiery man – a Hemingway figure or perhaps more a white African, as a student described him to me recently – with boundless creativity and the most original mind and hands I have ever come across. His paintings, sculptures and zoological texts were and are a testimony to what Africa was capable of inspiring and the kinds of phenomenal people it could draw to its breast and nurture. When we visit him and his ever-giving (though, thankfully, not uncomplaining) wife, Elena, in their cottage in Oxfordshire, the musings always meander towards those days at Makerere and the brief burst of fantastic light it engendered in all of our lives. It is funny to be sitting in shireland eating Elena's matchless Italian food and being so immersed in the images and memories of Africa. I love them both and hope to God that if I die before him, Jonathan's booming voice will say a little something over my coffin.

The happier and more unfettered I felt, the more easily I learned. The less I was put upon, the more I took it upon myself to make something of my academic abilities. But I also suffered fear. I knew that I simply had to succeed better than many of my peers because I never wanted to depend on anyone again (and I never have) and I had no big family money to catch me if I fell. My son is lucky enough to have the first of these in his life, but not the second. Will that make him less driven to succeed or will he push himself anyway because that is what he has seen his mother do all her life? Maybe he will want to win because he is a child of the eighties in Britain. That would be very disappointing even if it means, as he says, he will have his first million by the age of thirty.

Kanubhai ran the canteen where we all gathered for morning coffee and samosas. He had one ear and was so avaricious (well, he wanted to be paid all his cash at the point of purchase) that we unkindly used to put it about that, given the right amount of cash, Kanu would sell anything, even his own organs. He had that long-suffering air that you see on newsagents who are unfortunate enough to be near a secondary school. Notices were stuck up everywhere, most warning you not to ask for credit and to behave 'decently', his favourite word. He was incandescent with disapproval when he saw an Asian girl holding hands with a boy in his canteen: 'Shame has gone from our girls. Too much education is the problem. Just no *izzat*, like prostitutes, just like prostitutes and the African girls.' Strictly speaking, offensive though these outpourings were, there was some accuracy in his observations. We were not prostitutes, but he was right, shame had gone from us and probably because we were more educated than was good for us in a society which so needed conformity to give it a solid and eternal base.

I know I was perceived as someone who had gone (damagingly) native once I entered Makerere, especially when I decided to share quarters with Sophie and Jane. I delighted in this reputation, as long as it did not leave the campus. My family would find that hard enough, but Sky's family – which was far more conventional and whom I wanted to please more than anything else in the world – would have found it confusing to say the least. They liked me, some even loved me, and I repaid this by going to mosque every Friday, wearing saris and even a demure expression and by making the grandchildren wonderful cakes and clothes. My mother was shocked and pleased and a little hurt at the transformation. (She tells my friends now, a little triumphantly, 'She never came to the mosque with me, but with Sky's family she did everything and look now, what they did to her, they didn't care.') And although I too have felt grossly betrayed by them, I know, in my heart, how painful they have found what happened to our lives. How could I have expected them to do anything other than what they have always done, to stand by each other? And at one time I admired that very quality. The love Sky's mother and I felt for each other is preserved, even though neither of us can activate it for fear of the anger and hurt it would cause in others. I spoke to her recently on the phone after I heard she had been ill. We both wept, and I wept even more when she generously asked me to take my daughter, the child of the man who replaced her son, to visit her.

Sophie was tall and big, with a laugh that could fill a largish room. She is still so much like that. Only these days in the middle of some funny story which has me gasping with laughter, she remembers her husband who was killed by a gang of Amin's soldiers when her son was only two, or the way Obote's men tortured and slowly burnt her father to death, or how her only daughter died in 1994 of AIDS. Black Ugandans have been through so much more than Ugandan Asians. At least we could escape the terror. She and I met up again after I went to Uganda and tried to find her and Jane. An article in the local newspaper described my search and I had dozens of calls. Some were other old college friends I had never even bothered to worry about, but who had never forgotten that 'Asian fire bomb'. A few called only to say that they were delighted to find at least one of us coming back not looking for decayed buildings and long-lost businesses but long-lost and missed friends. I liked myself hugely that day and even more when I went to drink at an African bar for the first time in my life. (For all my attempts at being one of them, I had never before been into one of these bars, mainly because deep inside I must have thought they were dens of vice and disorder.)

Sophie, I found out, had been living in London all these years. How can I describe the emotions generated by our reunion? We loved each other. She and I had once talked deep into the night, she in her relative wisdom telling me what was what, and especially urgently about the brandy and hot bath solution should anything ever go awry with my early and inept sexual experiments. When I told her the story that I had heard in the mosque – how when a woman who was having an affair tried to abort the child she was carrying she was punished by giving birth to a baby who looked like a goat – Sophie laughed very loudly and disrespectfully. She and Jane would vacate the room for hours at a time so Sky could sneak in without being noticed by the warden – an upright, maybe slightly uptight English lady with a dog. I would shout at the other two because the room was always full of little fluffy tufts of hair which had burnt off while being chemically straightened. They hated the fact that the day I ironed my hair (yes, I wanted to look like Jean Shrimpton even more than I thought I already did) long strands would lie in the washbasin too. I was accused of being spoilt because we all had servants to pick up after us.

Jane was stunningly beautiful with eyes that always appeared slightly tearful. Her downfall was Anton. Until he turned up she was suitably detached and cool and surrounded by men who swore to die or kill for her. This was an accolade because at that time at Makerere there was no shortage of ripe and lovely African women wanting as good a time as the men had always had. But denial is a sexy thing and Jane was soon the girl with the most love notes left on the noticeboard downstairs. We shared clothes, which meant we had twice as many to choose from than when we had arrived. Sonali, a first-year medic, said to me once in her sweet, girlish voice: 'You know you must be careful, wearing her clothes. These people don't have the same standards as us.' We never spoke again. One of the reasons was, I said, that I could understand where her stupidity was coming from. Her father was an illiterate gold merchant who hired the son of a poor man to write out orders for him.

Anton was Californian, black, small, with a tight body, the emaciated sort that one caught sight of under tie-dyed T-shirts wherever the flowerpower children were hanging out, waving their arms, in the pictures we saw on Ugandan television, usually when a pro-communism politician was going on about the degenerate West. Anton was on a varied menu of drugs and he was downright nasty. Like so many black Americans who had swarmed into Africa at the time, he said he was looking for his real place in the universe and yet thought nothing of referring to Jane as his 'jungle bunny' or other Africans as 'barbies' – barbarians. Jane was captivated and felt unusually lucky to be asked to give this worthless man money, love and sex. Sophie and I openly hated him, and his comments on my 'nice butt' only added to my overdeveloped sense of disgust. I didn't meet Jane when I returned to Uganda, but I did hear that she was in the United States, a mother of six children. I only hope to God they are not Anton's and I am too scared to write to find out. 'Jane, are you foolish or what?' This is Sophie talking: 'That man is not even an African, Jane what are you doing? Opening your legs and purse for him? Sister be careful, I am telling you.' Sophie is always telling you.

Although I had never been as pious and dutiful as any of my Asian friends, long warning lessons, and the internal regulating mechanisms installed early on, made sure that I went quite close to the edge but never quite crossed over into really shocking behaviour. I was and am too much of a coward to disappoint or infuriate my people. Besides, I had seen how my father's rebellions had in the end left him alone and also felt the anguish in my family when my sister was lost to us for such a long time.

But I didn't go to the small student mosque every evening, I didn't wear unassuming dresses that fell below the knee and covered your upper arms, I didn't refuse alcohol with a shudder and I didn't stick to my own, although it was with somebody from my own community that I struck up a friendship which to this day means as much to me as my two children do and which possibly will outlast even their attachment to me.

Ferial (though I have always written it Feriyal, much to the annoyance of all those others in her life who have a greater claim to her than I do) was sitting on a bench outside Mary Stuart Hall one evening at dusk when all the faithful were off to mosque. I was sitting on the opposite bench. The girls all asked us as they went by whether we were coming. When the same question is asked, even mildly, fifty times, you can feel appallingly guilty. In her checked shirt, jeans and glowering expression under thick glasses, Feriyal looked tough and alone. When the others had gone we started chatting about the 'problems with religion'.

We had and have nothing in common except those anti-religious sentiments. And even that has changed somewhat. She is increasingly alarmed at my newish habit of taking a *tasbi* (rosary) to bed, and the long conversations I tell her I need now to have with a god, any god, my god before I go to sleep. I find it incomprehensible that she has bought into the American dream, which is a nightmare for so many. We fight, we barely understand the world the other lives in, but our love remains stubbornly steadfast.

She was a medical student, shy, self-conscious about the fact that no heads would turn to look at her except quizzically. She was convinced that she was irredeemably ugly, mostly because of the scars of some terrible acid burns on her legs sustained as a baby in her father's pawnbroking shop. In fact she was attractive and soon won the heart of an idealistic young American backpacker by whom, three children later, she is still adored. These days, however, she knows that she deserves this and a whole lot more. American positivism can indeed perform miracles.

In some ways she has not changed at all. Obdurate and indifferent still to the way she looks, it is her teenage daughter Sarah now who punishes and tortures her the way I once did. Goodness, those yells that rushed through the corridors of the ninth floor at Mary Stuart when two of us pinned her down and, singing 'Georgy Girl,' started thinning her ample eyebrows which she has since allowed to regrow, a bigger mess than before. Or the day I swore I would kill myself unless she wore one of my dresses and came to the pictures with Sky and me. When she saw herself in the polka-dotted frilly frock, my death was her preferred option.

She is perhaps now my only real touchstone, my link with the past as I remember it at Makerere. We only had two years to build up a friendship, but it has survived until now partly because it is based on something irrevocably lost which we need to keep alive by always talking about it.

That is why the end of my first marriage cuts so deep too. Our history at home and here has never been adequately recorded. We were holding all the stories, the pictures of our adopted country, the mad contradictions, the many languages which had leaked into each other to produce the most imaginative hybrid mix, and, most important of all, a sense that affection and obligation went together to produce in all our relationships a sense of permanence and continuity. Perhaps the eternal state of being migrants, never safe, produces a special need for those bonds because in the end that is all we have. Or had.

16

The sanctuary that Makerere had become made many of us turn a blind eye to what was happening out there beyond the walls. Town and gown living apart again. The times we did venture out, we saw the growing and now perfectly acceptable abuse of Asians, especially on the streets. They were, as always, the ordinary people, those who could not cut themselves off from the reality of what was going on by flashing by in fast cars and into their grand offices and houses, with their expensive sunglasses and *askaris* to protect them from the glare of animosity and envy. Peculiarly, these people were still venerated by the Africans, who found it easier to pick on the poorer Asians and punish them for the sins of their more affluent brethren.

In the market now, it is the Africans who would refer to the Asians as *shenzis* and *chors*, thieves. Fear was making the Asians obsequious and they would feign smiles and pretend these were jokes in order to reduce their misery a little. It was bitterly pitiful to see this. Once, a black man holding a chicken started taunting me about the *wahindis*. I lashed out at him and told him what I had heard Asians muttering amongst themselves and what I thought I never believed: 'You fool,' I shouted, 'where would you be without us?' Whereupon he threw the large clucking chicken at me and said, 'Be careful. One day we will force you to have our children.'

To make matters worse, the British government was passing increasingly hostile regulations which denied Asians with British passports any automatic right to enter their mother country. Quotas were brought in at the same time as Ugandanisation policies were being pushed through in all sectors of the economy. Every day, in the heat, a long line of exhausted and hopeless people would wait outside the British High Commission, not daring even to go for a piss in case their moment arrived and they were given five minutes to plead their special case to British officials who treated them, us, like so many items of garbage. They would mock our accents by speaking to us in Peter Sellers Indi-talk, they would ask us why we lied so much, and if you didn't speak with an accent, they found other subtle ways to put you in your place. As one self-styled poet, not of any great talent, wrote in his little book: 'our souls crushed between two cruel stones, the sweet juice was squeezed out'.

Just looking at the High Commission building again in 1994 made me break out into a sweat.

Then, suddenly, my brother became the victim of these 'two stones' in the most frightening and public way. Obote by this time was looking for an excuse to attack the British government and expose the hypocritical and dishonourable attitudes it was displaying towards its Asian subjects. He was doing this not out of any concern for us but to win on the propaganda front. He was handed victory on a plate by a British diplomat with his heart in the wrong place for the job he was meant to be doing.

Brian Lee was one of those whites who was too close to the people he was meant to despise. Just not a pukka sahib. He was charmed (some say bribed) by a group of British Asians who befriended and persuaded him to take up their cause. One day, the world woke up to the shocking news that a British diplomat had been kidnapped in Uganda. It was Lee. Within a couple of days, fear turned to fury as it was discovered that this well-meaning man had allowed himself to be taken off as part of some inept plot to fake a kidnap by a gang of Asian men, desperate to have their plight revealed to the world.

When ransacking Lee's home, the police found evidence that my brother, who had a travel agency, had sold him some tickets and had Lee illegally deposit the money in London. More evidence that the president could use to show the world that, for all their pinstriped suits and supercilious claims, the British were as corrupt as they said the Africans were. My brother was arrested and driven away and for days we did not know where he was or if he was alive. It was then that I realised how deeply I loved him still and how much his life mattered to me.

A few days after he was taken away, in his pyjamas, we nearly lost Farah. Crime was rising in the city and *kondos*, armed thieves, were everywhere. Often they were policemen, discarding their uniforms after hours and turning to a second occupation to supplement their meagre wages. Farah, still a toddler, was in the car when my sister-in-law went to lock up the business. The car was stolen with the child in it, and her mother, who was dragged along as she tried to open the door, ended up with the skin almost torn off one leg. It was the only time I saw Zarin cry and the only time I wanted to hug her. I didn't.

Farah was found several hours later in a village outside the city and brought to the police station by a kind taxi driver who saw her weeping and feared for her life. So hard had people now become that it would, he thought, have been possible for them to vent their anger even on a young Asian child. I did not believe this, because in East Africa children were always safe and although many black children were later caught up in the violence, I feel that what happened in Rwanda could not happen in the country where I was born and reared, and looked after with such tenderness by Ugandan ayahs. Farah still recoils if you mention the incident and black men did not fare too well in her imagination for many years to follow.

A week after this episode, my entire family was deported

from Uganda. They could take nothing: my brother was not even allowed to see his flat, the one he had spent years saving up to finally buy. My parents, and his family, were simply put on a plane and sent off, almost a century after our ancestors had arrived to make their home in a country which in the end was denied to their descendants. Even now, around the world, many of these lost children of East Africa are slowly going mad as they fail to come to terms with their loss.

I decided not to go with them, hoping that the authorities would fail to connect my name with that of my family especially as I didn't live at home. I was so deeply in love, it had made me foolishly heroic. My brother and mother were enraged and also petrified that if I was found out, the consequences would be unimaginable. But, as ever, I did not listen and even announced selfishly that I would get married if there was any threat of discovery, which made my family feel quite justifiably that I was no longer even remotely connected to them, that my heart now lay with Sky and his family, and that I did not care what was going to happen to them.

They were bound for England with no money, and only a gang of unpredictable cousins – that lot from Mwanza – who would promise the earth but would deliver in their own time and inimitable way.

And I truly didn't care, not even about my beloved mother or my young niece and nephew. I can make no excuses for this careless disregard now. The power of excessive love for a man can monstrously distort human behaviour.

They were all gone. I was as happy as I imagined a lark would be if the saying was to be believed.

Papa did not survive even a few months in Britain. The doctors could not tell us what it was and concluded that it must have been something 'tropical'. I think the England he saw in 1970, so utterly chaotic compared to the 1940s and 1950s, must have broken his spirit. I can't even imagine his horror at seeing the streets of his precious upright England littered with purposeless people lounging around in their halter necks and hideous bell-bottoms. He also, I suspect, had to confront what my sister had gone through during all those years when he had banished her and her daughter (the child that none of us, except my mother, properly embraced as our own and who now goes from success to success) from his life. I wonder how much of all this pain is locked tightly inside my sister. For years now she has often looked so occupied with thoughts and melancholy, chain-smoking, in another place and time. No longer even able to paint the beautiful little pictures she once did. These days there is a little more light in her eyes when she sees Leila, my daughter, a child she loves so much that she rings twice as day, hungry for news about what she is doing. I don't know what she went through in the years before I met her again. That is her story and I hope she can tell it one day. Meanwhile she lives in the dark and gloomy valleys of the Rhondda, with her fond and caring husband, Mick; like Colin, another Englishman. Sent by the heavens to care for the ones she loves, says my mother. Just before his death, my father sent me a postcard which simply said 'From Papa', his first act of real communication with me since the *Romeo and Juliet* fiasco. Too little, devastatingly too late, as they say.

At his funeral, Woking it was, in November, the moment that caused my eyes to flood was the tinkle of the spoon of holy water on his frozen lips. My brother was sobbing, my mother passed out after a series of fits, the kind she used to have all those years ago when I sat on her and held down her arms. We were all drenched in rain and grief which came out of a shared sense of utter waste and the impossibility of redemption, and that feeling has grown over the years. That must be why my brother compulsively visits the grave – which once was overrun with weeds – and tries to win his father's love, at least in death, and why my mother talks about him almost at times with a kind of reverence. Before he died, he apologised for making her life so hard, and that was enough for her.

I can only confess to missing what we might have had. And I am relieved that he never lived to experience the racist attacks and white contempt that so many of his generation have had to learn to tolerate since they came here. For him, the personal hurt would have been compounded by a deep disappointment that those he had considered, all his life, to be the most civilised people in the world had turned into such brutes.

I went back to Uganda a week after the funeral. (That was all the very suspicious British immigration officer was prepared to allow: 'There are always funerals and weddings, madam. You'd be surprised how many in one family and how many times over.') Already I felt I had been away too long and was not really aware of having been in England at all because our mourning rituals are so all-consuming.

Three months later, on 25 January 1971, to the tune of 'My Boy Lollipop', which was played the whole day long, a sombre voice of a soldier announced that there had been a coup in Uganda and General Idi Amin Dada was now the president. The transition was seamless. Obote was paying the price for offending Britain by his disdain at the Commonwealth conference in Singapore that year and, more dangerously for him, shamelessly flirting with the communist bloc. He found himself replaced with a smoothness that revealed how you are only really as independent as the big powers allow you to be. The Bagandans danced in the streets, the students at Makerere rejoiced by taking a few days off lectures and making daytime love, and the British and the United States instantly recognised the new regime, thinking that they had an illiterate man who loved the queen and who would, like a captive bear, dance to their tune more easily. How terribly mistaken we all were.

Soon afterwards, I realised how differently we were beginning to be treated. It was as if a certain protective threshold had been crossed. When coming back from a trip to Nairobi, I felt an unusual amount of apprehension, even terror. At Entebbe there were scores of soldiers hanging around, looking bored and menacing – a lethal combination. I was walking through when a gruff customs officer took it into his head that I was smuggling money. I explained to him that I wasn't, but that in any case that would not be breaking any law. It was taking money out that was the problem. Exposed as a fool – some of the others began to laugh at him – he started shouting that he would march me off to prison and actually jostled me and audaciously started pushing my long fringe away from my face. I burst into tears, he felt strong and powerful again, a few (Kenyan) shillings changed hands and I was out of the airport feeling much less as if I had arrived home.

Back at Makerere, I noticed more ominous signs that people were beginning to feel the dancing on the streets had been foolishly premature. Good sense was prompting more and more students to live within a self-imposed curfew. There was no more kiri-kiri music in the main hall, the bar emptied early and caution was making people refrain from too much socialising. 'You never know,' Sophie would say, 'when you might meet a gang of rogue elephants in the grounds.' You learned to whisper even when you were inside your own rooms, because general mistrust was growing that there were spies at the university. A heavy silence had descended on the hill. How can people in free countries understand how easy it becomes not to say the wrong thing?

Then the night raids started. Suddenly at about three o'clock, we would hear heavy jackboots striding up the many stairs and walking around. For the first few times, they did nothing but wander about and we found ways of using washbasins and makeshift pots if the need to go to the loo got unbearable. Those box-shaped glass lampshades are perfect if you can wrench them off the ceiling, and you knew how to pee accurately.

Then one night Mary and her twin sister Esther, students of agriculture and perhaps too well known for their sense of fun, disappeared. People on their floor had heard a muffled scream, the lift going down and nothing more. Eight days later, Esther came back, leaning against the pillars, barely able to walk and completely unwilling to talk. Rumours said that both sisters had been taken to the barracks and gang-raped for days and that

Mary was in hospital with a severely ruptured anus and bleeding nipples. A few days later Esther went back to her village, just months away from her graduation. The two of them would have been the first in the family to get degrees. All their relatives, including grandparents, had worked for years to pay for their education and their mother had not yet finished making their graduation dresses when all their lives were torn up by men embarking on their first wave of bloodlust.

There was worse to come. More jackboots purposefully wandering around the corridors, doors being kicked down and women's screams followed by an awful silence were heard, sometimes every night of the week. Soon it became clear that it was the Bagandan women who were the victims. Again the only reason, like before, was that they belonged to a tribe which the president was determined to coerce and silence, preferably for ever. At dawn many women silently packed their bags and left. Others attempted desperate but pathetic measures. Putting up Asian names on their doors or hiding in our rooms at that time ironically gave them some protection, because strangely the soldiers never approached us.

In the midst of this there were happenings so bizarre that you had to laugh. In an insane kind of way. A handsome student who was a newsreader on television was taken every evening by soldiers in a jeep to the studios to read the news and then returned when he had finished. This was in order to protect him. One night his protectors, laden with drink, decided to sport with him a little. One of their guns had been silent for too many days, they said. They wanted to use it. On him, but they wanted him to choose the spot. He thought quickly and before horror had turned his words to gibberish he chose his left foot. They shot it and then, roaring with laughter, drove him to hospital.

People in the town were suffering even more. Servants would no longer go back home at night and instead chose to sleep on the kitchen floors of the families they worked for. The soldiers were quite literally going beserk on the streets and the pride and hopes of a nation turned into silent dust. People did not dress up; they walked with their heads bowed, cowering before the irrational might of Idi Amin and his acolytes. He would suddenly appear and start directing traffic or more often stop it altogether as he went around with that infernal and eternal smile on his face. A friend whose uncle had had his genitals mutilated and fed to a dog by Amin, confirmed that the smile never left that large, puffy face.

Desperation among the Asians was growing too, especially those with British passports. The goldsmiths had never had it so good as people frantically began converting their cash into heavy, badly made jewellery. Most popular were ugly necklaces, bracelets, rings and earrings made of 21-carat gold coins which looked like guineas. Gold which looked like old English money was more reassuring than the intricate flowery designs we had loved previously. Unfortunately when these were worn, discreetly during wedding parties with the doors firmly locked, we all looked like wannabe mayoresses. Holes were dug in floors, special shoes which had cavities were made, jackets too, all to hide the pile of gold. This industrious concentration on protecting precious property kept our minds off the other dangers around our lives.

Sky graduated in 1971, and armed with a remarkably impressive degree in zoology, started allowing himself to dream the impossible, of Oxford no less, as the next step. His external examiner, a benevolent chap who looked like Groucho Marx and wore fuchsia-coloured shirts, was an Oxford man. He said he would be happy to have Sky as his postgraduate student. Overcome with pride and indebtedness, his family invited the examiner to lunch and then realised what they had done. None of us had ever eaten in our homes at the same table as a white person, let alone a man from Oxford. It was a delightful though extravagant occasion, what with the new tablecloth and posh matching cutlery, plus the anxiety of how to lay the table and do all the right things in order to convince this gentleman that we were worth the trouble he was putting himself through.

An enormous obstacle was unexpectedly put in the way of this grand plan. There was some panic at this moment that too many bright people, especially scientists, were leaving the country. Makerere offered Sky a job and research facilities, and he heard through the grapevine that his passport would be confiscated so that he could not leave the country.

The very next week secretly, and with some trepidation, he flew out of Uganda, leaving me behind to finish my degree and somehow survive without the support I had come to rely on almost entirely. He had replaced all the male affection that had cruelly gone missing in my life. The grip of this love was tight and strong and its passion fierce and dazzling. I longed to be with him so very much I knew then that he was the man I wanted to marry and live with for the rest of my days.

He flew into a Britain which was in the middle (or muddle, perhaps) of three-day weeks and power cuts. He had hardly any money and no friends. For the eight months we were apart, he wrote every day: about the cold, the custard creams and baked beans he was living on, and also the beauty of Oxford and how small that could make you feel. I was dying to get out there. Uganda was fast losing its lustre and allure.

In October that year, Amin made one of his many speeches at some barracks, denouncing Asians, ordering a head count and calling us Jews, whom he hated. He claimed Asians were 'sabastaging' the economy and refusing to marry Africans. Sex and money lay at the heart of his growing resentment and our growing fear. Not many of my African friends seemed to condemn what Amin was saying and I realised that I too was rising to defend my people wholeheartedly even though I knew and had felt that we had not always behaved honourably or with respect towards the Africans. Personal relationships can give you deep insights but they are not enough to disengage you when battle lines are drawn. As ever we, the Asians, started creating even more drama out of this crisis by a flurry of rumours which could feed our sense of panic. Amin was on a crusade of vengeance, it was claimed, because he had been spurned by an Asian woman, the widow of the most prosperous Asian industrialist in the country, Jayant Madhvani. Apparently she refused to become one of his many wives. If they could have, most Asian fathers would have locked up their daughters with the other precious objects they had been hiding.

At university, the one incipient love affair between an Asian woman and an African man which had been tolerated, if not encouraged, now began to be seen as the unacceptable face of integration. They parted, feeling unable to carry the conflicts of an entire nation.

Things were becoming precarious for us. Two Asian men were killed by soldiers at a petrol station. No one story of the incident was the same as the next. Howls of sorrow from the mosque filled the night skies. People were crying for more than two departed souls. Bribe brokers began to appear, people who claimed to know this minister or that, or better still, a British immigration officer. Hasmukh, the chubby, good-natured fellow I had been to school with, became a kind of godfather overnight, commanding reverence because he knew people in power and loving every minute of it. He used to be in awe of brainy girls and the last time I met him still showed me a huge and undeserved amount of respect. I hear he is now a tycoon in Bollywood, still driving around in a white Mercedes. Diasporic gossip like this keeps us all enthralled and in touch even though much of it is out of date. Six years after my divorce from Sky I still have to cope with the deep disappointment of somebody we once knew turning up from Nebraska or Saskatchewan and saying with genuine sorrow, 'Oh *yaar*, I just did not know. Believe me, it is this life in the West. Why didn't you tell me? You are my sister', as if we still all live but a bowl of biryani away from one another.

It was 1972, the president was continuing to make ominous noises about the greed of the *wahindi* and people were watching and waiting. With my finals approaching fast, I stayed in my room, in my spotted pink pyjamas, working and pining and being mopped up by Feriyal when it all got too much to bear. She would come back from the teaching hospital nearby, Mulago, once the pride of Africa, with horrific stories of how many maimed and murdered civilians were being brought in to be patched up until the next time or wrapped up in plastic bags under the cruel eyes of the soldiers.

We were getting so frightened that there was a day when we both thought it might be an idea to start going to mosque, just in case . . . Unfortunately they no longer opened the college mosque for fear of drawing attention.

I remember doing my finals in a kind of haze. With so much palpable danger around the place, and feeling that you were living through an acutely important moment of history, it seemed too petty for words to worry about how I had done in the drama paper.

I passed with a flying first and had serious talks with one of my tutors about how one day I would end up in his office, on his chair imparting to the new, eager-eyed generations of Ugandans the joys of literature. I packed my precious records and books and left them with a friend in town. I was getting ready to leave, but only (at least in my head) for three years. I knew I wanted to live and die in Uganda, although for the moment the thought of going to Oxford, surely the heart of greatness, especially with Sky already there, had gripped my imagination.

PART 3

1972–1975

Please try to be clear, dear James, through the storm which rages about your youthful head today, about the reality which lies behind the words *acceptance* and *integration*. There is no reason for you to try and become like white people and there is no basis whatever for their impertinent assumption that *they* must accept *you*. The really terrible thing, old buddy, is that *you* must accept *them* . . . for these innocent people . . . are in effect, still trapped in a history which they do not understand.

James Baldwin, in a letter to his nephew
The Fire Next Time

17

It was June. I bought a ticket, pearl necklace and black velvet dress with the money I had earned working in a shop in the vacation. Many tears were shed as I left Makerere and there was more weeping at the airport as I said goodbye to my surrogate family and Feriyal. But anticipation dried those tears soon enough.

The plane was full of bewildered people who had finally got their vouchers to enter Britain. I believe the older people, at least, were as reluctant to do this as the British were to receive them. Both sides had deluded themselves that the blue passports were a way of maintaining their status and lives in East Africa. Both were shocked that these meant nothing any more. The younger people on the plane were more enthusiastic; more naive too. The plane was permeated by the fragrance of mangoes and pineapples, and the more pungent smells of pickles and *chevro*. We were travelling cheap, on Air Sudan, which felt obliged only to serve jam and rock-hard bread rolls every few hours, together with sweet milky tea. No one seemed to mind one bit as the Tupperware boxes and shiny tiffins were opened up and food shared around to go with the tea. I was snobbish (and stupid) enough by this time to decline to participate in such crass, low-class ways. There were five passengers without seats. They sat in the aisles or on seats offered to them for brief rests.

There was endless chatter, about the relatives in Leicester, the small business plans, how unspeakably awful Uganda had become. An old woman sitting next to me was crying because she was moving to the UK with her daughter not her son, who had turned away from her after his marriage. She had left her teeth behind in the rush to the airport and she wanted to know how much it would cost to buy a replacement set. I said I did not know, but that general dental treatment was free over there. A shaft of relief spread over her face. She did not want to be more obliged to her daughter, because she was already guilty of sin, living off her.

And so we landed and queued up to face irritated white officials, having left the appallingly rude black ones behind. Tottering on my high heels, I walked out and fell into the lusty arms of my husband to be, who was thinner and more pensive than he should have been.

We got married soon after I arrived. It was a bigger wedding than either of us wanted and one which my brother and his family could ill afford. But they understood and we didn't how important it was to keep up respect and pretence and not just send off your sister to her marriage bed without at least some kind of public show. They did it because they felt they had to do it and their resentment leaked out in all sorts of ways. Perhaps they would have been less full of pique if we had appreciated them better. Dressed in a pure white sari, looking like a slightly fleshy Indian actress, with flowers in my hair and devotion in my eyes, I looked and played the part of a virgin bride, even touching the feet of my parents-in-law. My husband looked like an escapee from the Grateful Dead band in a purple suit, long curly hair and a droopy moustache. There we are, in the photographs, the couple of the decade, cavorting in Hyde Park, feeding each other *laddus* at the reception in a grim school hall in Harrow with candlewick bedspreads used as tablecloths, looking utterly awash with joy and hope.

Our student flat was on the top floor of a house in north Oxford. We had one small grant to live on and I could not cook at all. For months, we had frozen hamburgers topped with tinned pineapple, wrapped in bought pastry, even converted into lumpy bolognese sauce. The treat was Kentucky Fried Chicken, which I still love. Meanwhile, my mother, now convinced that I was indeed an educated girl, was finally imparting some of her impressive cooking skills to me, via the phone, or on painstakingly written bits of paper whenever we met. The rest of the house had the usual sort of characters, mainly women: Susan, a bluestocking and earnestly Christian, Amanda, a bulimic who stole food and who looked like she was a member of the Addams family walking about with incense sticks in her hand, and Kathy, my first friend in England. Her bright and warm personality and the ease with which she took us into her lives was more important than she will ever realise, and although she now lives in grand, upper-class style, something of that early receptive innocence remains, thank God.

All the women adored Sky and he basked in it. (It was not a bad time to be a handsome oriental in Oxford even if you weren't quite Tariq Ali or the son of a dispossessed maharaja.) This was an excellent way of getting him to fix hairdryers and broken heels. These were the children of the sixties, of course, many of whom genuinely did not appear to have any of the arrogance of the white people we had met at home.

I was full of very good feelings about myself and sent in my application to do my MPhil in Lit. with no self-doubt at all. The Prince's Foundation was persuaded by Mrs McPherson that I was, like my husband, a truly worthy cause and I knew it was only a matter of a short wait until I too could, with panache, get into one of those punts and drift away to dream of the glorious future.

And then suddenly, a few weeks after our marriage, Idi Amin announced that Asians with British passports had to leave the country. At first we hardly reacted at all, believing this to be a kind of sick joke by a man who was no buffoon but who loved to bait the Asians to distract attention from his own gruesome activities. Soon and very quickly, it became apparent not only that he meant business, but that all Asians were to be expelled and that the Africans were ecstatic at the prospect, believing that they would all then be rich and drive around in big cars. It was an expedient move, a PR strategy by a leader whose dreadful deeds were becoming too well known. But it was not only the insane act of one megalomaniac. Although it has never been easy even to accept this, most black Ugandans backed Amin, and the Asian community, through its refusal to change, had in a way helped to create an atmosphere where they were not wanted any longer. We shared a dreadful responsibility in denying all our children a future together. My in-laws had not yet paid for the ticket to attend our wedding when they had to pack up again. But they had nowhere to go because they were Ugandan citizens.

We never felt the atmosphere that developed in Uganda at the time, except at a distance and through the British media. But I remember the terrible pain of watching my people being treated like cattle, tripped over, kicked and shoved as they boarded buses outside the Nita cinema, their whimpers and tears as they left carrying the little they were allowed, leaving behind all their posessions, the things that had given meaning to their lives for generations. (On my return visit I went to this cinema which is now closed down, and across one fading poster advertising a Hindi film, someone had scrawled 'Go to hell, Uganda'.) Sky's family had no wealth to carry out except a few bits of jewellery and Ugandan passports which were worthless. We were frantic with worry and helplessness. In the end people like that were to be luckier than most, because Canada airlifted them to make new lives over there and they have all prospered beyond their dreams. Most still pine for the country of their childhood, though, and among those who have gone back to Uganda you do find many of these Canadians who have made huge amounts of money but are still searching for a homeland.

Those who arrived here were much less welcome of course

and it was agonising for us to watch the confused faces of people as they emerged, dishevelled and exhausted, from the airports to see groups of grim butchers from Spitalfields screaming at them to go back. We saw, and threw away with fury, huge newspaper adverts telling people not to go to Leicester because it was too full of Asians already. We listened to the educated voice of Enoch Powell talking about us as if we were vermin. And worst of all was the way people were expected to show enormous gratitude to Britain for being allowed into their own country. We were not refugees. We were British. This is something that no British politician has properly acknowledged. When I interviewed Sir Edward Heath in 1992, even then he loftily told me: 'Few other countries helped us with this problem, so we had to take them. The British people have a reputation for looking after people. We were very careful to get them to a wide variety of places so they would be spread out.'

The only time I have been seriously violent in my life was one day in November 1972 when a weedy little taxi driver threw my money in my face when I told him I was from Uganda. I grabbed his hair and pulled it, pushed the coins into his face and ran off.

I visited one of the refugee camps near Oxford. In some ways it was extraordinary how a group of people who had lost everything could still sing together when they were cooking and laugh at their own childlike terror of what was going to happen to them. The men, in small groups, would be talking of how to get started, bank loans, how to exploit any tenuous connections with people who had already settled.

Mithi (meaning sweet, a nickname her husband gave her on their wedding night), a forty-year-old mother, was the most traumatised person I met at the camp. She had a British passport, her husband a Ugandan one. She had been allowed in, he was in India with their eldest child. With tears rushing down her face, Mithi kept walking around in just a cotton dress and rubber sandals, with a *tasbi* in her hand. She asked me if I could help her to prepare a feast for seven virgins. I said it was probably not going to be easy in the camp. This is a last-resort ritual used by the desperate in our community when troubles seem too much to bear. You gather seven pubescent girls, preferably from less well-off families, you feed them, fuss over them, and send them off with lovely white lacy handkerchiefs and rose water. I was always a very popular choice back home. Mithi would not be persuaded that in the cold, damp camps with dormitories and institutionalised conditions, she could not purge her sins in this way and get her husband to join her. It was fifteen years before they could be together again. By that time, Mithi had turned grey and sour.

You had to sit and listen endlessly to the tales of loss, always at this time expressed in terms of homes, cars, furniture, gold. Later the longings changed, and people would reminisce about the weather, the Ugandan landscape, the servants. There were also the fears about their children growing up in a country which was, when it came to sexual behaviour, *besharam*, without shame. How proudly they would react when I told some of them I was at Oxford.

In small ways, they started finding solace. In sweetmeats from Southall (although they would complain these were never as good as they could make them), in Hindi song cassettes, in pictures, statues of various gods and fervent prayers; in recreating the kinds of network which gave the community cohesion in Uganda. The one thing that delighted and comforted all the families was the education that they felt their children would get in a country they admired for more than anything else.

Those who hated to be dependent got down to it immediately. Kamrubhai, a close friend of my family, a man who had never wronged a person in his life and who was loved and respected deeply by all of us, found a job lifting huge boxes in a department store. He was already middle-aged, and at home would have been living his *badshai* life. It broke my heart to see what he was going through, but he never once complained about the work. Hard work was in their blood, and this, in the end, saved them from destitution and degradation.

My brother lived in Ealing at this time and I remember his fury when we were passing the town hall and there were white people shouting and thrusting their thick fists in the air, complaining that too many of us were ending up in their borough. One of these men, Ken, now dotes on his beautiful Ugandan Asian daughter-in-law, Deepa, and says he is sorry for the way he behaved then. Deepa, a friend of mine, was seven when she arrived and she does not let anyone forget what she was made to feel. She stopped eating for months, had to go into hospital, nearly died. All, she says, because she was so frightened when she was pushed and shoved by black soldiers in Uganda and then came out of the airport here expecting to be safe, only to confront more angry men who didn't seem to like her either.

Somehow though, as more and more of this started happening, the two of us, unconsciously I believe, started dissociating from the people who were always portrayed as pathetic, broke, incapable of communicating in English, backward. I did feel guilty when I felt myself shrinking away from my people, especially after I had visited a resettlement camp and seen their degradation. Here, these entrepreneurs, the offspring of pioneers, were treated like children by many of the ex-colonials who were managing the camps.

For those first few years, many of the people I knew lived in cramped rooms, fifteen, sixteen people sometimes. They had no heating, they could only bathe every other day, using small plastic bowls and cups. They watched the agony of their elders pining for home, they learned to live with an enforced humility that they felt was the only way they were allowed to behave in this hallowed country.

But although I could feel sympathy and anger for the new arrivals, I was desperately keen to show people that I was not one of them. I remember travelling with my mother on a bus in

London and a ticket collector being abusive to her. I turned my face to the window and pretended that we were not together even though she had paid my fare. Living in Oxford, it was easy to cut yourself off, to luxuriate in the sequestered atmosphere. So I bought a Laura Ashley Victorian gown and a hat with flowers and sat under apple trees reading George Eliot. I learned about cream teas and cider, and Sky took up croquet. We had become English, we thought, even though we were given plenty of hints that many around us weren't entirely convinced by our metamorphosis.

My tutors, for example. In fact I should have known. When I went for my interview one supercilious gentleman suggested I should go to 'Leeds or somewhere like that' because I said I was interested in V. S. Naipaul. I had read more widely than any of them, but they always left me feeling less worthy than any of the other students and although they let me on to the course, most of them behaved as if they could not for a minute understand what I was doing in their midst. My tutor had little to say to me (and eventually I reciprocated) though he did one day ask me kindly whether I misspelt Michael because I wasn't English. The man who taught Wordsworth seemed to consider it a profanity that someone who was not profoundly English should be studying nineteenth-century literature. This was all done in the most civilised way, of course. It is amazing how hurt you can feel when you discover that you are the only student who is never offered a sherry during tutorials and never invited to Sunday lunch.

At college we had a moral tutor who was duty bound to provide pastoral care. Ours studiously ignored us, even during the expulsion crisis when it was quite clear that we needed help and support. Years later, when I met him at a reunion, I asked him very loudly whether he had been paid for this responsibility which he had never carried out. The shock for both of us was that I was able to say this to him and he, a handsome arrogant man, turned into sweetness itself for the rest of the evening.

But that courage came later, much later in life. I worked like a dog when I was at Oxford, and got my MPhil but my love for literature and my intellectual confidence were demolished. I hated those suave students who always spoke as if they held the only possible right opinion on all matters and it was only later, in the dead of the night, thinking about another day when I had failed to open my mouth that I realised that so much of what had been tossed out as great ideas was simply bosh.

Other aspects of my personality flourished though, and this was largely due to the fact that our college, Linacre, was a newish post-graduate college which had no great pretensions and actually took pride in the fact that it had such an international student community. It had to be modest I guess, because it was such a wee small building right next to the imposing spires of Christ Church. The Senior Common Room chaps couldn't and didn't attempt to distance themselves from us and social popularity was not hard to come by. Especially if you could dance well. Our principal was a tall, thin man who was alarmingly clever and charming and who could establish his superior position without ever straining too hard to do so. Born to govern: some people are, and they can do it so naturally that there really is no time to mind. The two men below him evoked far more irritation in all of us. Somehow they were too intimate, too crude, and lacking in dignity. And when we threatened to strike against the expensive, bad food that the temperamental chef was serving up, some of our actions were aimed at upsetting those who didn't have the class to rise above it.

But it was the students who made the atmosphere of the college. There was Anus (pronounced Anoos), who said he was the son of a Muslim prophet and who was insanely in love with a Lebanese temptress. He followed her at a respectful distance until giggling, she would disappear into the changing rooms of Selfridges. Later, a Roman Catholic priest was similarly ensnared. In fact, this being the seventies, you were surrounded by talk, music and thoughts about sex. In Africa so much less was said and more done about it.

There were startling transformations, and not just in the sons of prophets. One woman friend, who had arrived in Linacre looking like a chaste nun, in weeks was walking around with an exposed midriff and on the arm of a rather promiscuous American who looked like a beautiful horse. She was the only one there who could dance better than I could. There was a Welshman who pulled the birds by emulating the degenerate lifestyle and seductive lilt of Dylan Thomas. Few of us failed to succumb to his charms.

So here we were, a married Asian couple, strictly brought up, and wayward only in a tame sort of way, surrounded by free sex, drugs and rock 'n' roll. What made it so electrifying was that there was no guilt, no shame, no censure. It felt like Babel on a fine day. We declined the drugs and (mostly) the real sex, but we did learn to play wild games, to flirt shamelessly with whatever came our way, to appear one of the crowd and, I think (and this was the destructive bit), to cease believing in self-control and decency. We were overwhelmed that we could be included and not at all upset when we weren't, which did happen in subtle ways.

Here is a scene that often comes to mind. Sky is playing croquet with great style and success. Three others are playing too and one is Brian, this big English bloke with an awful lot of misplaced self-love. He is wearing a leather hat and trousers and seems only ever to talk to the other two. He asks if they want a beer. Sky, who is at this point still a teetotaller, tells him he'd like a Coke and conspicuously hands him some money. I am furious at both of them, and in a crude display of hurt and anger I tell Brian later that he is a rude bastard. I feel inordinately brave. He laughs, grabs my arm, and kisses me on my face as if he owns me and all the space around us. I feign outrage, but inside I feel flattered and excited. An Englishman's kiss, for the very first time in my life.

By now the last traces of colonial humility had disappeared

and I think we were trying to grapple with the responsibility of developing more equal, more natural relationships with white people. Such transitions are not easy. And it was indeed madly exciting to know that you could turn men on who were once your masters. Is this why I wore that grey and wine-coloured suede miniskirt to the Bodleian and made sure my knickers were pretty so that I could climb the step-ladders with confidence and watch the pallid, bespectacled men looking up at me? Or why so soon after we were married, Sky felt drawn to a woman with long greasy hair, who wore the same calico skirt every day, lived in a squat and whose smell lingered in a corridor long after she had passed through?

The combination of liberation from the past and the mood of the early seventies was making us throw caution to the winds, talk enthusiastically about open marriages, discard all the deeply important values we had been brought up on. And some things, if thrown far enough away, are impossibly difficult to find again.

We did try and manage, especially after we had had our son, to live a life which could incorporate much that was good in this society and also what we had, for a while, chucked away so casually in our days at Oxford. But when Sky left he was talking again about self-indulgence, gratification and free love and I understood then how pervasive and corrosive some of our early experiences in this country had been.

But Oxford, especially Linacre, also gave us wonderful meaningful friendships most of which have lasted all these years and did compensate hugely for the loss of our home and country. Only one or two of these friends have since failed to be there when I needed them. One, who is especially missed, could not, would not take sides when my marriage broke up. Such neutrality seemed to me either cowardice or betrayal, for it is not true that there are always two sides to everything, and true friends are not equivocal. Some people cause hurt and break hearts and others are their victims. This Christian view (my friend was a lapsed Catholic) based on exculpation and easy salvation can only encourage destructive behaviour. He could not fathom what I was on about and I could not forgive him. And for an exile, a migrant, the friendships made in the new afterlife are hugely meaningful (even more than the first double bed and TV set you buy when you have settled) and you feel their loss acutely and for a long time.

Then there was Brean, my clever Scotsman, a Pepys in some (not all) ways, whose beautiful handwriting, wit and intelligence won a chunk of my heart and he keeps it still. We spent hours in coffee shops where he would educate and provoke me and I would banter with him, knowing I would never match his erudition but that he would never hold that against me. The intellect can be such a very sexy thing. No touch needs to be exchanged, but the excitement generated by the heat and fecundity of a person's mind can last much longer than that other, more mundane kind of sexuality. But, though we were both doing English, even with Brean I never dared to discuss Literature. And I so wanted to, especially when I read 'Tintern Abbey' and felt I would burst with pleasure because finally I could get to grips with a poet I had assumed was too English for my imagination.

Our children are now friends, and this is how you weave a new life into an old country and make it yours.

Friends like these and a growing sense that we belonged made much of the time spent at Oxford, at least socially, very nurturing. It is true that the cost of this was detachment from our own people. How can I otherwise explain why I felt so exposed and embarrassed when I got on a bus with my mother who then spoke very little English? Or why I felt a chasm between myself and my old friends and did my best to avoid being with them? Or why I insisted on wearing clothes that always showed too much leg (much much more than at home), cleavage and almost the whole of my back? It was great to have people saying what a beautiful colour my skin was but that could not have been the only reason.

Although shame has tarnished things now, at the time all

that we felt was how wonderful life was. And it was, especially when I learned good Indian cooking and could use that too to entice friends. I remember cooking puris for a group of about twenty in a lovely cottage outside Oxford. The antique table I was rolling them on suddenly swung down and turned into a Victorian love seat. We could not get the table back so my fourteen puris stayed in there and even now must be slowly festering.

Sky was working on voles at some nearby woods, a colony that had been studied endlessly by others. It must have seemed depressingly domestic and tame to a man who had spent his life surrounded by the wildlife of East Africa, but for an Oxford degree it seemed worth it.

We were incredibly lucky in so many ways: gifted in how we could relate to other people, ultimately engrossed in each other, and far away from the anguish and turmoil that the other 'refugees' were going through, sheltered from the worst taunts and slamming doors. Disgracefully privileged, really.

Perhaps the most fortunate thing that happened to us was that we found the Blaschkos, two people who proved to be the family and voices of wisdom that we needed at this time. It was 1973, we were homeless and they had a student flat upstairs in No. 24, Parktown. Incredibly generously, they let us have it for almost no rent and it was our home for nearly six happy years, until I was four months pregnant with our child.

Hugh Blaschko was seventy-three then, a world-famous scientist, with a curiosity, intellect and passion that did not leave him until the day he died in 1994. Humility was his other great strength. His wife Mary filled all of our lives with kindness and unconditional love. Both could keep you entranced with stories, whether they were about the time Hugh was forced to flee his native Germany and cope with the deaths of many of those he knew and loved – unimaginable horrors – or the robin who visited the tree outside in the garden every day at the same time. Mary was and is especially good on the various people who had inhabited the Parktown crescent, including a

Pasternak, many Toynbees and their cats, and other salubrious beings who were reduced to nice or perhaps not always very nice ordinary folk by her tales. But perhaps the greatest debt I owe them is the lesson Hugh taught me about how dispossessed people lose much less than they gain, that not having a nation, a country, a flag, is a liberation which enables you to see, feel and taste the whole world as an insider. I think that is what he meant when he emphatically said that the diasporic destiny thrust upon European Jews, excruciating though it was, was the best thing that could have happened to them.

That and the example of what a relationship can be. Their marriage, though childless, was half a century long and enviably happy. Mine with Sky didn't even make it to the half way mark. But I pray, many times a day, that I will grow old with Colin and that we too will fumble and stagger around in our ember days irritating, teasing and adoring each other the way I saw the Blaschkos do.

Epilogue

When I went back to Uganda in the summer of 1994, a funny thing happened on the way from the airport into Kampala. I saw a woman selling fruit at the roadside. After twenty-two long years, it was my first sight of those enormous pineapples, mangoes, papaya, jackfruit, fruit that when bought and eaten in England had never tasted the same. I asked our driver Douglas, a charming young man of twenty-two (he was just born when we left Uganda), to stop the car so I could buy something. A small child, perhaps three years old, started screaming as she saw me approaching. I tried to stroke her face and the screams only got louder and more real. The mother told Douglas, her eyes looking down with shame, that her daughter was frightened because she had never seen a brown face before.

This is the new reality of Uganda, where most of the young have never lived in close proximity to Asians, where they have only the vague stories about who we were and why we left buried somewhere in the rest of the bloody history that has passed through the country. The older generations of course do remember only too well. For some the return of a few Asians is seen as reconciliation and a chance to move on. Others are afraid that the same old inequalities will emerge and their dusty capital will be reclaimed again. Nobody wants the past back as it was, not even the most hostile Africans nor any of the Asians I met, although a few have started to behave arrogantly and are having to be told that automatic servility is no longer available to them. But many of us have learned hard lessons in the West, and that is making us properly humble. Fewer blacks these days boast that they can do it on their own. And that humility in both groups is leading to a new kind of mutual respect. That may be the best news in a country where in the places where there was carnage, the flowers are finally beginning to bloom again. Even more encouragingly, a crane holding a huge boulder which has been suspended over a busy street for twenty years was finally creaking back to life, the day I left. If political disorder can be kept in check and the soldiers behave themselves, if the returnee Asians genuinely help to rebuild the country, the people of Uganda may finally see their hopes realised, decades after independence.

On their own version of *Desert Island Discs*, I was asked on a Ugandan radio station if I would come back to live in Uganda. I hope so, I said, but you get tired of moving. What I do know for sure, though, is that I will go there to die.

Glossary

achaar	Indian pickles, usually made with mangoes and chillis.
aree	An expression of surprise or disappointment (Gujarati, and Kutchi).
askari	An East African security guard or policeman (Swahili).
ayah	A maid who looks after children.
babu	A young boy (Gujarati and Kutchi).
badshai	Luxurious, lordly (Gujarati and Kutchi).
bai	Sister, often added to the end of names to show respect.
baksheesh	An offering of money, like a tip or to a beggar (Swahili).
banyani	A slightly offensive way of describing Hindus used by other Asians and Africans.
besharam	Without shame (Kutchi).
beta	A term of endearment used by older people for those younger than themselves (Kutchi).
bhai	Brother, often added to the end of names to show respect (Kutchi and Gujarati).
bichari	An expression that shows sympathy for someone, a bit like 'poor thing' (Kutchi and Gujarati).
boy	A male domestic servant in East Africa.
bwana	The master (Swahili).
chacha	Your father's brother or cousin (Kutchi and Gujarati).
chachi	Your father's brother's wife (Kutchi and Gujarati).
chevro	A savoury snack of fried lentils and nuts.
chor	A thief (Gujarati); used by black Ugandans too.
choroko	Dhal or lentil curry (Swahili).
chotara	Offensive word to describe mixed-race children of an African/Asian alliance.
dhoko	A large wooden stick used to clean clothes when washing them.
dholki	A white woman (Gujarati and Kutchi).
didi	Endearing term for an elder sister on the subcontinent.
dukanwallah	Small shopkeepers selling general goods, often in remote villages.
Eid	The two annual Muslim festivals.

ghar jamai	A son-in-law who lives with his wife's family. Generally something that is frowned on (Kutchi and Gujarati).
gola	An offensive term for a black man used by East African Asians.
gungru	Dancing ankle bells (all Asian languages).
hajj	The annual pilgrimage to Mecca by Muslims.
hijab	The head covering used by many Muslim women to comply with the requirements of modesty in the Koran.
Holi	A Hindu festival celebrating life when people throw coloured water at each other.
izzat	Amongst Asians, the idea of family or personal honour, usually thought to be in the hands of the women.
karanga	Peanuts (Swahili).
kasookoo	A parrot (Swahili).
kisrani	Bad luck (Swahili).
kitenge	Cotton fabric wtih African designs worn by women across Africa.
kondos	Armed robbers (Swahili).
kuba	Big (Swahili).
Kutchi	A dialect spoken by people from northern Pakistan and the province of Kutch in India.
kuthi	Bitch (Kutchi).
laddu	Sweetmeat eaten at weddings.
maama	Your mother's brother (Kutchi and Gujarati).
maami	The wife of your mother's brother (Kutchi and Gujarati).
maasa	Your mother's sister's husband (Kutchi and Gujarati).
maasi	Your mother's sister (Kutchi and Gujarati).
mama	The way servants addressed the women they were working for.
mascheed	A mosque (Hindi and Urdu).
maskini	A beggar (Swahili).
matoke	A savoury green banana, eaten cooked, one of the staple foods of Uganda.
matoongi	A clay pot to store or carry drinking water (Swahili).
memsahib	The mistress: used commonly across East Africa.
mogo	Cassava.
Mohorrum	A period of annual mourning by certain Shia Muslim groups to atone for their part in the killing of a religious figure.

moong	Moong beans, small green beans commonly used in Indian vegetarian cookery.
mwalimu	Teacher (Swahili).
namaaz	Muslim prayers, often performed by the devout, five times a day (common in most Asian languages).
nasib	Luck (Kutchi and Gujarati).
oudh	A strong-smelling perfume product used by a bride on her wedding night. It is burnt on coals and the bride sits near the fumes until her skin takes on the scent.
panwallah	A man who sells pan (small edible leaves containing betel-nut and other chewy bits usually eaten after a meal to freshen the mouth).
paya	Goats' trotters.
Pyar	Love (all Asian languages).
rotlis	Chappatis (Kutchi and Gujarati).
saitan	Satan (Kutchi and Gujarati).
sala	A slightly mocking way of addressing somebody who has failed to do the right thing. Used with another more offensive word, it becomes more biting and insulting (Kutchi and Gujarati).
sanene	Large green locusts (Swahili).
shalwar khamiz	Loose trousers and long tops worn by people from India and Pakistan.
shanti	Peace and quiet (Gujarati and Kutchi).
shenzi	Fool, barbarian (Swahili).
soovar	Pig (Gujarati and Kutchi); used as a swear word.
tasbi	A rosary used by Muslims.
tiffin	A metal container with several compartments to carry food to work or on a journey.
tobah	An expression that shows horror and a lack of fear of God (Kutchi).
wahindi	Asians (Swahili).
waragi	An alcoholic brew made by local Ugandans from sugar cane.
wazungu	White people (Swahili).
yaar	A term used by friends with each other; an expression of friendly intimacy.